Henry Faulkner Darnell

Songs by the Way

A Collection of Original Poems for the Comfort and Encouragement of Christian

Pilgrims

Henry Faulkner Darnell

Songs by the Way

A Collection of Original Poems for the Comfort and Encouragement of Christian Pilgrims

ISBN/EAN: 9783744704687

Printed in Europe, USA, Canada, Australia, Japan

Cover: Foto ©Thomas Meinert / pixelio.de

More available books at **www.hansebooks.com**

SONGS BY THE WAY:

A COLLECTION OF

ORIGINAL POEMS

FOR THE COMFORT AND ENCOURAGEMENT OF

Christian Pilgrims.

BY

THE REV. H. F. DARNELL,

RECTOR OF ST. JOHNS, C.E., AND ACTING CHAPLAIN TO THE TROOPS.

DEDICATED TO HIS PARISHIONERS.

"The ransomed of the Lord shall return, and come to Zion with songs."—
Isaiah xxxv. 10.

Montreal;
PRINTED BY JOHN LOVELL, ST. NICHOLAS STREET.
1862.

PREFACE.

The Author presents this little volume to the public with a prayer for the Divine blessing, without which it can never be successful after the manner that he desires. He makes no apology for its issue, inasmuch as he considers it a duty incumbent upon all, to serve their generation to the utmost of their ability. Most of the poems were composed amid the urgent and manifold duties which devolve upon a parish pastor: in some cases they were suggested by incidents which presented themselves in the course of parochial visitation, whilst in others they express the actual experience of the writer. Should they, notwithstanding their defects, afford those who peruse them half the pleasure and comfort which he has himself experienced in their composition, he will be perfectly satisfied.

The Author has ventured to dedicate this, his first work published in Canada, to those who are nearest to his heart, viz., his Parishioners in St. Johns. He sincerely hopes that at least it may bring no discredit upon a community which has manifested towards him the utmost kindness and cordiality; and for which he has already learned to cherish sentiments of such affectionate regard.

RECTORY, ST. JOHNS, C. E., 1862.

INTRODUCTION.

"The ransomed of the Lord shall return, and come to Zion with songs."— Isaiah xxxv. 10.

How often does the weary traveller, returning homeward from a distant country, love to beguile the solitude and tedium of his journey with snatches of song; which at once give utterance to the feelings within his heart, and cheer and stimulate his flagging spirits. The strains naturally vary according to the different emotions which reign within his breast. Whilst sinking under the fatigues of the way, and far off from his destination, they are of a mingled, and chiefly of a mournful character; but, as he nears the home where loving friends are waiting to welcome him with open arms, they give expression solely to the joy and happiness which fill his bosom.

Even so does the *Christian* pilgrim, as he treads the rugged steep which leads to Zion, gather solace and encouragement from song, in which he gives vent to the emotions struggling within him, and thus lightens the heavy load under

INTRODUCTION.

which he bends. The burden of his song takes its complexion from the condition of his soul, and from the ever-changing circumstances by which he is surrounded. At the outset, he mostly chooses such strains as excite his courage and devotion, and rouse his dormant energies; or else such as remind him of the comforts, privileges, and helps placed within his reach. In notes of praise and thanksgiving, he frequently has occasion to acknowledge the favor and protection of a beneficent Father. In the hour of trial and weakness, in strains of fervent "prayer and supplication, his requests are made known unto God," and His aid is invoked. When his spirit passes under the cloud, and is oppressed with a sense of sin and spiritual darkness; when he has experienced some crushing calamity; or when he has committed the lifeless form of some beloved friend to the silent dust;—he finds it an unspeakable comfort, in suitable and touching strains, to give expression to the feelings of humiliation, grief, despondency, hope, and confidence, as they successively dominate within his heart. But, as he advances on his upward way; rises above the cares of earth, and catches sight of the golden gates, his songs become more joyful and triumphant; till at last, as he treads the golden streets of that heavenly city, and all its glory bursts upon his view, no earthly strains can give utterance to the rapturous joy which fills his soul; for nought but an angel's harp and an angel's tongue can declare the unutterable bliss of the accepted saint, as he stands in the presence of his God and his Redeemer, one of that ever-blessed band of whom the prophet speaks: "the ransomed of the Lord shall return, and come to Zion with songs and everlasting joy upon their heads; they shall obtain joy and gladness, and sorrow and sighing shall flee away."

Permit me then, dear reader, as a fellow-pilgrim, bound for the same celestial city, to touch my harp and sing my songs within your hearing. You may be farther advanced than I on the road to glory, and your spiritual experience is, I trust, deeper and sweeter than mine; you may oft be basking in the sunbeams of the Divine presence, whilst I am yet but struggling through the clouds and mists which float between it and this lower world; yet I am in hopes that the utterances of my heart may sometimes wake a response in yours, and minister, in some slight degree, to your comfort and encouragement.

Should I find one fellow-pilgrim in *heaviness*, and leave him in *peace;* should I find but one brother *wandering*, and be enabled to lead him back again to the *narrow way;* should I find one fellow-sinner *without a Saviour*, and leave him *at the feet of Jesus;* neither they nor I will ever cease to rejoice that I fell in with them during their journey, and with feeble hands and feebler voice, sang to them these 'Songs by the Way.'

CONTENTS.

SONGS BY THE WAY.

		PAGE.
1.	The Beaten Path,	11
2.	The Walk with God,	13
3.	Church Membership (in five parts):	
	The Christian Covenant,	18
	The Sabbath and its Services,	19
	Confirmation,	20
	The Lord's Supper,	22
	Death, Burial, and Resurrection,	24
4.	Earth-written Names,	26
5.	I'll follow Thee,	28
6.	Afloat,	29
7.	Christian Friendship,	30
8.	The Narrow Way,	31
9.	Invitation to Early Piety,	33
10.	Sabbath Morning Hymn,	34
11.	Sabbath Evening Hymn,	36
12.	'Lord, teach us to pray,'	37
13.	The Ocean Sabbath,	39
14.	A Child of the Kingdom,	41
15.	The Woman that was a Sinner,	43
16.	Flowers and Ears of Corn,	47
17.	Faith,	49

CONTENTS.

	PAGE.
18. Living Temples,	50
19. "Deliver us from evil,"	53
20. Look to Jesus!	54
21. The Christening of the First-born,	56
22. The Death of the First-born,	58
23. "Thy will be done,"	61
24. In Memoriam,	62
25. "I will not leave you *comfortless*,"	64
26. Elegy,	66
27. Life,	69
28. Sunset Reflections,	70
29. Things Beloved,	71
30. The Family Bible,	73
31. Incentives to Praise,	76
32. A Mother's Hymn,	77
33. Bochim,	78
34. No more Death,	81
35. The Æolian Harp,	84
36. The Coming Year,	86
37. Seed-time,	88
38. Seasons of Prayer,	91
39. Under the Snow,	93
40. In the Trough of the Sea,	95
41. "Bear ye one another's burdens,"	98
42. My Church,	101
43. Smiles and Tears,	103
44. Heart Treasures,	104
45. The Proto-martyr,	106
46. Light in Darkness,	108
47. United Prayer,	112
48. Spiritual Longings,	116
49. Days that are gone,	118

CONTENTS.

	PAGE.
50. The Old Man's God,	119
51. On to Glory!	122
52. Homeward bound,	123
53. To-day and To-morrow,	125
54. Departing in peace,	127
55. Looking for the Evening,	129
56. Night and Morning,	131
57. Pisgah,	133
58. The Promised Land,	136
59. Is it well?	138

DETACHED POEMS.

1. The Widow of Nain,	143
2. The Work and the Workers,	151
3. The Death Signal,	157
4. The Emigrant's Departure,	159
(A Scene in Ulster, A. D. 1853.)	
5. Chimes of the Sea,	162
6. Havelock's Grave,	166
7. Memorial of Macaulay,	170
8. On the Decease of the Prince Consort,	173
(A. D. 1861, ÆT. 41.)	
9. The Faithful Steward,	175
(Written in commemoration of Mr. George Peabody's parting donation of £150,000 to the poor of London, in which city this Christian-minded merchant amassed his vast fortune. The donor was born in Danvers, Massachusetts, U.S., and in humble circumstances.)	
10. On visiting the tomb of the late Rev. J. B. Ob. A. D. 1855.	179
11. The Pioneers,	182
12. Inscription for a Time-piece,	186

SONGS BY THE WAY.

THE BEATEN PATH.

"Thus saith the Lord, Stand ye in the ways, and see, and ask for the old paths, where is the good way, and walk therein, and ye shall find rest for your souls."—*Jer.* vi. 16.

The sands of life drop day by day,
Pilgrim, inquire the heav'n-ward way!
Tread, tread the path that Jesus trod,—
The only path that leads to God.

Oh! see how many round thee lie,
Whose soulless forms are mould'ring nigh;
They rest for ever as they fell,
The *saved* for *heav'n*,—the *lost* for *hell!*

The patriarchs of ancient years
Have journey'd thro' this vale of tears;
Unnumber'd saints this path have press'd,
With weary feet, and found their rest.

THE BEATEN PATH.

Martyrs have left their crimson stains
On these rough heights, and thorny plains;
Unawed on earth by tyrants' frowns,
Their brows now gleam with living crowns.

Then murmur not,—" The path is steep,
My soul is weary, and must sleep!"
There scarce is time to pause for breath,
There is no *sleeping* but in *death*.

Complain not that the way is drear,
Full of suffering, full of fear;
But, halting Christian, ope thine eyes!
The thorns are flowers in disguise.

What joy lies hid 'neath gushing tears!
What hopes beam bright 'mid darkest fears!
And, ah! when worldly cares increase,
What blessed springs of heav'nly peace!

On, fainting pilgrim! onward go!
Look not for pleasure here below!
Deem not this earth a place of rest,
But seek a Saviour's loving breast!

THE WALK WITH GOD.

"And Enoch walked with God: and he was not; for God took him."—Gen. v. 24.

How solacing amid the cares
Which Earth's defilèd bosom bears,
To have some loved companion nigh,
Each pang to soothe—each tear to dry!
One on whose never-failing breast
The weary head may peaceful rest;
One who our joys will gladly share,
And, when our wounded hearts we bare,
Will bend with ever ready ears,
And weep with sympathetic tears,
At that accumulated woe
Which makes the spirit overflow.
No earthly gloom is then so deep
But, star-like, joys will thro' it peep;
No path so desolate and drear,
But flowers of comfort blossom near;
Whilst even sin's profound abyss
Is spann'd by hope of future bliss,
As he, like messenger of grace,
Leads us to seek the Father's face.

But where such love devoted gain—
Such sweet companionship obtain?

THE WALK WITH GOD.

Can we on *earth* such love secure
As shall thro' all its trials endure—
Provide a balm for ev'ry grief—
Meet ev'ry want with quick relief?
Ah! earthly friendship oft will fail
When dark and threat'ning storms prevail;
And those who sought us when the view
Glow'd bright with beams which Fortune threw,
Will leave us crush'd and trampled down,
When stern Adversity doth frown;
When men our names with mockery greet,
And tread our fame beneath their feet.
How hard from friends of happier days
To meet the false and stony gaze,
Which tells of kindnesses forgot,
And coldly says 'I know you not!'

And e'en with those who true abide,
Whom nought could tempt or fright aside;
E'en if of such a little band
Should seek to stretch a welcome hand,
Or strive our wounded hearts to bind,
And cheer us with their accents kind:
How oft some intercepting thing
Prevents the aid they fain would bring!
Now 'tis the distance vast between—
Now the dark waves that intervene:

THE WALK WITH GOD.

These separate e'en bosom friends,
And mar the solace Friendship sends.
Sometimes the heart on which we lean,
In ev'ry woe or sorrow keen,
Itself, all crush'd and bleeding, lies,
Needing our own deep sympathies;
And all unable to inspire
The peace and comfort we require.
Each has his diff'rent path in life;
Each has his own engrossing strife;
And friends, like streams by headland parted,
Must oft, forlorn and heavy-hearted,
Pursue their course, with sadden'd tone,
And thread Earth's wilderness alone.

And e'en when fond companions meet
To soothe with kindly words and sweet,
How many cares lie dark and deep—
How many woes the spirit steep—
Which burden'd souls cannot reveal,
Nor ministering Friendship heal!
Yes, there are wounds that thrill too much
To bear the tend'rest *human* touch;
Known to the heart its bitterness—(¹)
None else can fathom its distress!
But blessed they who, while they tread
This earth, with doubts and dangers spread,

---

(1) *Prov.* xiv. 10.

THE WALK WITH GOD.

Can yet lift up to yonder skies
Their aching hearts and streaming eyes,
And see, the gloomy darkness thro',
A Father, Friend, Companion too;
And who, with faith and patience shod,
Have learned betimes to walk with God!
When *man* their burden cannot share,
The '*everlasting arms*' are there:
Whatever friends be torn away,
That 'Friend of friends' shall ever stay;
The world may oft *our* hearts estrange,
But His affection knows no change.
No oceans can from Him divide;
No distance keep Him from our side;
His loving eyes shine on our way,
And follow us where'er we stray.
He knows the secrets of the soul—
He marks each wave of sorrow roll;
And sees each gnawing inward care
Which feeds upon the quiet there.
He marks each sinful thought and deed,
Which made His Son incarnate bleed;
And sees the misery and pain
That ever follow in their train.
He views the daily conflict waged,
The soul from earth more disengaged;
He marks the groan—the deep-drawn sigh—
The pray'r of faith—the tearful eye;

THE WALK WITH GOD.

And, as His tender soul doth melt,
He hastes to make His presence felt.
Before His cloud-dispelling smile,
Flee earth's dark cares and Satan's guile;
The pilgrim, late by gloom oppress'd,
All faint, perplex'd, and deep-distress'd,
Now sees around a cheering light,
And feels a superhuman might,
And, as the ruder tempests cease,
Soft-breathing zephyrs whisper peace.

Oh, walk, my soul, in that sweet way
That leads to everlasting day!
Set not thy heart on things below,
Look not for wreaths earth can bestow;
But covet that enduring treasure,
Seek that unalloyèd pleasure,—
That rest which for the just remains,
Where Jesus now in glory reigns!
Walk like to him, the saint of old,
Who, now among the bless'd enroll'd,
These weary wilds once meekly trod,
And early lov'd to '*walk with God.*'
Walk thus, that when upon thy sight
Death comes, enwrapt in gloom of night,
Thy Lord may banish all alarms,
And '*take thee*' to His loving arms.

CHURCH-MEMBERSHIP.

I.

"Suffer the little children to come unto me, and forbid them not; for of such is the kingdom of God."—Mark x. 14.

I saw a little infant child
    Borne up the sacred aisle;
I mark'd the father's look of pride,
    The mother's happy smile.

The pastor stood beside the font,
    And took that little one
All tenderly within his arms,
    As Jesus would have done:

He sprinkled on its brow the sign
    Of God's renewing grace,
And gave it in the church of Christ
    A title and a place.

It was a touching sight to see,
    And, oh! it thrill'd me through
To think not only we ourselves,
    But our dear children too,

Might enter into covenant
    With Him who reigns above—
Drink deeply of His saving grace,
    And share His tender love.

II.

"Lord, I have loved the habitation of thy house, and the place where thine honour dwelleth."—Psalm xxvi. 8.

Again I sought that holy place,
   And look'd for that sweet child;
Upon his fresh and joyous face,
   Some dozen springs had smil'd:

It was a calm, bright Sabbath-day,
   God's worshippers were there;
And, 'mid the rest, I saw his lips
   Move in responsive pray'r.

I heard he was a wayward child,
   With spirit high and bold—
With temper full of gen'rous warmth,
   Yet scarce to be controll'd:

Headstrong at times, yet easy led
   By accents soft and kind,
From those round whom his youthful heart
   With fond affection twin'd.

From such, e'en in his stormiest mood,
   One single look of pain
Would oft subdue his stubborn will,
   And make him mild again.

They told me too ' 'twas passing strange
    The deep, warm love he felt
For God's sweet Sabbath, and the House
    In which His honor dwelt.'

It was no longer strange to me
    Who saw him worship there,
And how he clasp'd his mother's hand,
    And join'd with her in pray'r.

No wonder that he lov'd that spot—
    That holy, happy day;
He nearer seem'd to her he priz'd
    When earth was far away.

III.

"Whosoever therefore shall confess me before men, him will I confess also before my Father which is in Heaven."—*Matt.* x. 32.

I look'd again within that Church—
    More years had roll'd away—
Its sacred doors are open'd wide,
    Again 'tis Sabbath-day:

Fast-gath'ring crowds come pouring in,
    And soon its courts they fill;
Whilst over all deep awe is spread,
    And ev'ry lip is still.

CHURCH-MEMBERSHIP.

There stands the pastor, he who feeds
　　The flock of Jesus there,
And, by his side, a holy man
　　With kind, yet rev'rend air.

There, set apart, is rang'd a group,
　　With meek heads bending low
In solemn thought,—and there I see
　　My friend of long ago.

My heart was anxious for the youth,
　　I knew his temper wild—
I knew that mother's hand no more
　　Was nigh to guide her child;

And thank'd my God, though she had left
　　Earth's cares for Heaven's joy,
The Church had still a mother been
　　To that poor orphan boy.

She sought him out with loving eye,
　　When youth is prone to stray,
And led his wav'ring feet once more
　　To tread the narrow way;

And now the vows which others breath'd
　　For him, in days long flown,
Are ratified before the world,
　　And firmly made his own.

With pray'rs and blessing on his head,
 God's aiding grace within,
He goes to fight the Christian's fight—
 The Christian's crown to win. (¹)

IV.

"The cup of blessing which we bless, is it not the communion of the blood of Christ?

The bread which we break, is it not the communion of the body of Christ?

For we being many, are one bread and one body; for we are all partakers of that one bread."—*1 Cor.* x. 16, 17.

"This do in remembrance of me."—*Luke* xxii. 19.

Ah! 'tis no easy warfare that,
 Which he was call'd to wage,
Many and fierce the foes which round
 The youthful soldier rage;

And there are traitors in the camp,
 Base thoughts the soul within,
With evil passions and desires,
 And longings after sin;

And, ah! the flesh is weak, although
 The will may yet be strong, (²)
And oft when striving for the right,
 We yield to what is wrong. (³)

---

(1) II *Tim.* iv. 7, 8. (2) *Matt.* xxvi. 41. (3) *Rom.* vii. 21-23.

What wonder then that soon I saw
   The young ' confirm'd ' draw near
To that sweet ' supper of our Lord,'
   To fainting souls so dear.

His quiv'ring lip and tearful eye
   Proclaim'd that faith was there,
And yet upon the fair young brow
   Were signs of holy care :

He had much wand'ring to regret,
   Much sin to be forgiv'n ;
And oft he mourn'd himself unfit
   For blessedness in Heav'n.

It was not the *material* food
   For which his spirit sigh'd,
But that celestial meat and drink
   Which there were typified :

The cleansing blood from Jesus' side—
   The sweet and Heav'nly Bread—
By which the soul's renew'd and wash'd,
   And for the Kingdom fed.

He came in deepest penitence,
   He knelt in fervent pray'r—
And none return thence unrefresh'd
   Who thus seek Jesus there !

CHURCH-MEMBERSHIP.

V.

"I am the resurrection, and the life; he that believeth in me, though he were dead, yet shall he live.
And whosoever liveth and believeth in me shall never die."—*John* xi. 25, 26.

I saw him last beneath that roof,
   In springtide of the year;
The sunbeams pour'd a golden flood
   Of light upon his bier:

The very Churchyard seem'd to smile
   Above her mould'ring bones,
And wild-flow'rs twin'd their fragrant arms
   Around her mossy stones.

But, ah! the mourners gather'd there
   But little solace drew
From all her sweet and winning looks—
   Their grief was yet too new.

And yet it seem'd to me 'twas meet
   To bear him to his rest,
When Nature look'd her loveliest,
   And Earth was gayest drest:

My sadden'd thoughts were led to dwell
   On brighter days in store,
When anguish shall not wring the heart,
   And death shall slay no more:

CHURCH-MEMBERSHIP.

When lifeless forms, bestow'd in faith
    Beneath the verdant sod,
Shall live again, and, glorified,
    Surround the throne of God.

Sleep on, material frame of one
    Now flown above the skies!
Sleep, till the trumpets' wak'ning note
    Shall summon thee to rise!

The Church in which thy parents first
    Their child to Jesus gave,
Shall stand a faithful sentinel,
    Beside thy silent grave;

And who shall tell, 'ere yet ye both
    Have sunk into decay,
But thou may'st see the glorious light
    Of Resurrection-day?

EARTH-WRITTEN NAMES.

"They that depart from me shall be written in the earth, because they have forsaken the Lord."—Jer. xvii. 13.

I saw a shipwreck'd mariner
    Cast on a sea-beat shore;
Wounded and chill, he sunk to sleep
    To wake on earth no more;
But ere his ransom'd spirit flew
    To its eternal home,
His dying fingers on the strand
    Traced out his name and doom.

But, ah! that record, brief and sad,
    No mortal eye could see;
The billows wiped it out, and bore
    His lifeless corpse to sea:
His comrades trod the very spot
    Whence fled his spirit fleet—
They knew not of the parting words
    He wrote beneath their feet.

I saw a mighty prince uprear
    A monumental stone,
Inscrib'd with deeds of glory wrought—
    With trophies proudly won;
I mark'd the flush upon his cheek—
    The kindling of his eye—
The glance of high defiance cast
    On land, and sea, and sky.

But, lo! the tempest rent its base,
    And cleft its shaft in twain,
Till now the puzzled traveller seeks
    Its history in vain;
For time's defacing hand hath swept
    That proud inscription o'er,
And none can tell whose bones lie hid
    Beneath that ruin hoar.

So perish those whose fleeting names
    And man-applauded worth,
Are written but by mortal hands
    On records of the earth;
Who, for the fading things of Time,
    Forsake a Saviour's love,
And seek no name, no place within
    The Book of Life above.

But, oh! how blessed they who feel
    That they are number'd *there*,
With saints now crown'd with living light
    And free from worldly care;
With those redeem'd from ev'ry land
    Where Heav'n's bright light is spread—
Whose names and worth shall live and shine
    When time and earth are fled.

I'LL FOLLOW THEE!

"If any man will come after me, let him deny himself, and take up his cross and follow me."—Matt. xvi. 24.

Lord, I am sinful, wav'ring, weak,
Thy gracious favor I bespeak;
I have no strength to stand alone,
What might I have is all Thine own;
Yet, through the storms that round me rage—
Through erring youth and feeble age—
Through ev'ry trial Thou may'st decree,
Lord, with Thy help, I'll follow Thee!

Through loss of friends, and failing health—
Through want of what the world calls wealth;
Through stripes, imprisonments, and chains—
Through gloomy forests, burning plains:
Through all the thorns that strew the way—
Through all that tempts the soul to stray;
Where'er Thy footprints I may see,
Lord, with Thy help, I'll follow Thee.

On through the shadowy vale of death,
Where mortals yield their parting breath;
On through the cold, sepulchral gloom
That shrouds the horrors of the tomb;
On through the glitt'ring spheres above
To glorious realms of peace and love,
Where white-robed angels wait for me,
Lord, with Thy help, I'll follow Thee!

AFLOAT.

"He bringeth them unto their desired haven."—Psalm cvii. 30.

Speeding along down the river of Time,
    Speeding along to Eternity's sea,
A gay little bark, in her beauty and prime,
    Dancing above the bright ripples, I see.

The sunbeams are gilding the waters around,
    And Fancy lights up the bright prospect before;
Whilst Ocean seems wrapt in a slumber profound,
    As light-footed zephyrs glide murm'ringly o'er.

Take heed, little vessel, be careful! beware!
    Nor tempt without pilot the treacherous tide;—
Where the waters are calmest and brightest, 'tis there
    Too often dark rocks of destruction abide.

Let not the soft breezes tow'rds Pleasure's sweet isle,
    Inflate thy white canvass, and bear thee astray;
Let not Ease and Folly thy senses beguile,
    But, true as an arrow, speed onward—away!

For the winds that now whisper will presently roar,
    And waken the billows which tranquilly sleep;
Till they rush with wild fury on every shore,
    And the universe echoes the wrath of the deep.

Be ready! be vigilant—thoughtful—and true!
    Place Faith at the helm, and set Hope on the mast;
Then dark clouds may gather, and wild waves pursue,
    But thou'lt reach a sure haven of peace at the last.

CHRISTIAN FRIENDSHIP.

TO A FRIEND.

"We took sweet counsel together, and walked unto the house of God in company."(1).—*Psalm* lv. 14.

Oh, what a charm doth Friendship lend to life!
   How dear a friend when Fortune's sunbeams glow!
But dearer far when adverse storms are rife,
   And sorrow's billows o'er the bosom flow.

What solace sweet his soothing accents bring!
   Oh, what a balm attends each pitying tear!
And death itself is robb'd of half its sting,
   If friendly forms still fondly linger near.

The simplest flow'r, if pluck'd by Friendship's hand,
   From Nature's bright and beautiful parterre,
Will lovelier seem, touch'd by Affection's wand,
   Than all the fairer, costlier beauties there.

Our friendship's seed sprang forth in boyhood's years,
   Ere we the rugged paths of life began;
Th' unfolding bud maturer age still cheers,
   And may its blossom bloom upon the man!

---

(1) "As friends;" Prayer Book version.

May each succeeding day, like Heav'n's bright dew,
    With soft, refreshing influence descend,
And bid it shine life's dreary journey through,
    With heighten'd beauties as we near the end!

Then, when the weary pilgrimage is o'er,
    Our souls, united in the bonds of love,
On seraphs' wings triumphantly shall soar
    And dwell with rapture in the realms above!

THE NARROW WAY.

"Strait is the gate, and narrow is the way, which leadeth unto life, and few there be that find it."—*Matt.* vii. 14.

Press on! fresh courage take,
Nor let thy feet forsake
    The narrow way:
Though many a flow'ret fair
May bloom in beauty there,
    Oh, let it stay!

Though wreath'd in smiles of joy,
Vice doth her arts employ;
    Oh, pass her by!
From pleasures bought by pain—
From Folly's gaudy train,
    Avert thine eye.

THE NARROW WAY.

Let not Fame, Wealth, nor Pow'r,
Companions of an hour,
   Tempt thee to stray;
Fix'd be thine eyes above,
Where beam eternal love
   And perfect day.

Thou hast a work to do,
A world to travel thro'—
   A world of pain;
But when thy race is run,
And thy blest home is won,
   How great thy gain!

There bliss and peace abound—
There sweetest joys are found,
   And pain's unknown:
There shall thy glad voice ring
With Angels, as they sing
   At God's high throne!

INVITATION TO EARLY PIETY.

"Remember now thy Creator in the days of thy youth."—Ecc. xii. 1.

In childhood's bright May-morning,
    In manhood's dawning prime,
Obey the sacred warning,
    And seek thy God in time!

Though all around be gladness—
    Thy youthful heart be light,
And tears of pain and sadness
    Have never dimm'd thy sight;

Though yet thy cheek be glowing
    With health's bright rosy beam,
And life's fair tide be flowing
    With clear, untroubled stream;

Let not these blessings given
    Excite thy spirit's pride,
Nor let thy heart be driven
    From thy dear Saviour's side!

On earthly joys and pleasures,
    Oh, place not thou thy trust!
These are but fleeting treasures—
    True joys are with the just!

SABBATH MORNING HYMN.

Disease may soon steal o'er thee,
   And sickness pale thy bloom;
Bright hopes may fade before thee—
   Thy sunshine turn to gloom:

Misfortune, pain, and sorrow,
   May blight the gayest heart—
The closing of the morrow
   The thread of life may part:

But Death no terror bringeth
   To the soul that heav'n-ward hies,—
Glad strains of joy it singeth,
   As it cleaves the starry skies!

SABBATH MORNING HYMN.

(For the Young.)

Though I am but a little child,
   I'll seek God's house of pray'r;
On little children Jesus smil'd,
   And loves to see them there.
His gentle, patient, loving face
   On earth I may not see;
But I can, at the throne of grace,
   Seek Him who died for me.

SABBATH MORNING HYMN.

My heart shall, like the fruitful ground,
    Receive His holy will;
His Gospel's sweet and sacred sound
    My ransom'd soul shall thrill:
My joyful lips shall sing His praise,
    As all His love I see,
And hymns of loud thanksgiving raise
    To Him who died for me.

And when, without His sacred walls,
    I tread life's thorny way,
Whene'er my God, or duty calls,
    I'll cheerfully obey:
Whatever path He bids me tread,
    This shall my beacon be—
Though clouds may gather overhead—
    "My Saviour died for me!"

Then, when my pilgrimage is done,
    And life's last day is o'er,
The narrow gateway will be won,
    And sorrow be no more:
For in His kingdom, face to face,
    The Saviour I shall see;
And in His glorious visage trace
    Jesus, who died for me.

SABBATH EVENING HYMN.
(For the Young.)

O Lord, the light is fading fast—
    The darkness coming on;
Another day of grace is past;
    Another Sabbath gone!
How have I kept Thy holy day?
    Have I my soul defil'd?
Have I forgot, in any way,
    That I am Jesus' child?

Ah! yes, O Lord, my restless mind
    Too oft was turn'd from Thee,
And often did the Tempter find
    Some weaker part in me;
Too often were my careless feet
    From Heav'n and Thee beguil'd;
But, Father, still, in mercy sweet,
    Look on Thy erring child!

Pardon each vain, unchristian thought—
    Each sinful word and deed;
And make me seek Thee as I ought,
    And feel how deep my need:
Bow down my stubborn will to Him,
    Who still'd the tempest wild;
And let my faith, though often dim,
    Still mark me Jesus' child:

That when the last great Sabbath day
   In fadeless splendor breaks,
My soul may wing its heav'nward way,
   As it to glory wakes;
And, one amid that joyous throng
   In garments undefil'd,
May praise the love in endless song,
   That made me Jesus' child.

LORD, TEACH US TO PRAY.

Luke xi. 1.

At smile of Morn, at frown of Night—
   Throughout the busy day,
Acknowledging Thy sov'reign might,
   Oh, teach us, Lord, to pray!

In poverty, or ease, or wealth,
   'Neath Fortune's fickle ray,
In hours of sickness or of health,
   Oh, teach us, Lord, to pray!

Not only, breathing words, to kneel,
   With hearts still far away;
But, fir'd with holy love and zeal,
   Oh, teach us, Lord, to pray!

LORD, TEACH US TO PRAY.

For sweet forgiveness of the past—
   Each lost or mis-spent day;
For mercy, should this be our last,—
   Oh, teach us, Lord, to pray!

For grace our wand'rings to retrace,
   To break from Satan's sway,
And live in peace before Thy face,—
   Oh, teach us, Lord, to pray!

For strength to follow Christ, our Guide—
   To tread His thorny way—
To stem the force of Pleasure's tide,—
   Oh, teach us, Lord, to pray!

That we may live a life of pray'r,
   And serve Thee night and day;
And when 'tis o'er, Thy glory share,—
   Oh, teach us, Lord, to pray!

THE OCEAN SABBATH.

" He maketh the storm a calm, so that the waves thereof are still Then are they glad because they be quiet."—Psalm cvii. 29, 30.

'Tis sabbath on the Ocean,—
    How solemn, yet how sweet!
Here only sky and water
    Around the pilgrim meet;
Yet what a noble temple,
    And what a holy calm—
The very breeze seems burden'd
    With the words of some sweet psalm.

'Tis sabbath on the Ocean,—
    Above her thousand graves
She slumbers, as if Jesus
    Had lull'd her heaving waves;
Whilst e'en the ruder spirit
    Of man is charm'd to rest,
As earth-born cares are banish'd
    Awhile from ev'ry breast.

THE OCEAN SABBATH.

'Tis sabbath on the Ocean,—
   How soft on wind and wave,
The notes of that blest Gospel
   Which God in mercy gave!
How tenderly they call us
   From scenes of earthly strife,
To seek, within His kingdom,
   Unfading crowns of life!

'Tis sabbath on the Ocean,—
   How sweet, O God! to find,
Though *home* has faded from us,
   Thou art not left behind;
But still art present with us,
   Amid life's saddest hours,
To typify so sweetly
   The peace of Heaven's bow'rs!

'Tis sabbath on the Ocean,—
   She has her darker moods,
And o'er the human spirit
   The storm-cloud often broods;
But now we may together
   Enjoy a brief repose—
Together feel the presence
   Of Him from whom it flows.

'Tis sabbath on the Ocean,—
  Bless God, my soul! for this,
And ev'ry blessed foretaste
  Of that far higher bliss,
Which waits the wayworn wand'rer
  Across the swollen tide,—
That bliss for which the Saviour
  Was born, and bled, and died.

A CHILD OF THE KINGDOM. (¹)

"Of such is the Kingdom of God."—Mark x. 14.

Youthful Pilgrim, come away!
  Soon thine earthly journey 's done;
By the dawning light of day,
  Thou thy heav'nly home hast won.
Few have been life's cares for thee—
  Thine a flow'ry path to tread;
Few the thorns thine eyes could see—
  Few the storms above thy head.

---

(1) The subject of these verses was a beloved pupil of the Author; and was remarkable for his pious, obedient, and affectionate character. He died at the early age of ten years.

A CHILD OF THE KINGDOM.

Youthful Soldier of the cross,
    Lay thine untried weapons down
Thine the gain without the loss—
    Thine an easy-purchas'd crown!
Short thy strife with deadly foe—
    Few the hardships laid on thee;
Few the mournful notes of woe
    Ere the shouts of victory.

Tender Lamb of Jesus' fold,
    Come! it is thy Shepherd's voice;
Come! His loving face behold—
    Seek His bosom, and rejoice!
Nought can vex or harm thee there—
    Nought can tear thee forth again;
Through sweet pastures, bright and fair,
    Thou shalt follow in His train.

Young Disciple of the Lord,
    Earthly studies now are o'er;
Thou shalt hear God's holy word
    From lips of mortal man no more:
But there's a happy, holy place,
    Fill'd with blessed saints above;
There shall Jesus, face to face,
    Shew thee of His boundless love.

THE WOMAN THAT WAS A SINNER.

Weary Pilgrim now at rest—
Soldier at the Conq'ror's board—
Lamb within the Shepherd's breast—
Lov'd Disciple with thy Lord :
Such is now thy glorious lot,
Such for ever shall it be ;
Clouds of earth can dim it not—
Thou art in Eternity !

THE WOMAN THAT WAS A SINNER.

Luke vii. 36 to 50.

Low at the Saviour's feet
A guilty sinner bends ;
Up to his loving face
A tearful glance she sends :
" Can one, Himself so pure,
Of lineage so high,
The loathsome sight endure
Of one so vile as I ?"

Around His weary feet
Her loving arms are cast,
Whilst tears of sorrow sweet
Fall o'er them thick and fast ;

THE WOMAN THAT WAS A SINNER.

    Her long and flowing hair—
        The pride of woman's eye,
    Is not esteem'd too fair
        To cleanse and wipe them dry.

How doth each warm caress
    Her clinging lips impart,
In language mute express
    The yearnings of her heart!
That ointment rich and rare
    Her poverty could bring—
Its odours sweet declare
    'Tis no mean offering.

The Pharisee and Scribe,
    Exalted in their pride,
Can gaze in silent scorn,
    Or turn their eyes aside;
Can gather up their robes,
    And feign a pious fear,
Lest they should be defil'd
    E'en by her passing near;

But from "the Sinner's Friend"—
    Her gracious, loving Lord—
No scornful looks descend,
    No proud, no angry word:

THE WOMAN THAT WAS A SINNER.

" Can he a prophet be,"
　　Their wond'ring looks would say—
" And suffer such as she
　　Within His sight to stay ?"

" Yes, sepulchres of sin !
　　Who, whited fairly o'er,
Are dark and foul within,
　　And rotten at the core ;
Yes, His keen gaze can pierce
　　Each human bosom through,
And to His searching eyes
　　She's purer far than you !

" She whom the righteous spurn—
　　Whom Publicans revile—
Whom sin's most loathsome marks
　　Deface, degrade, defile;
Though on her guilty soul
　　Be many a deep, foul stain,
Her faith in Jesus' blood
　　Shall wash it pure again !

" But you—your lengthy pray'rs,
　　Hypocrisy and pride,
Long robes and public alms,
　　Your God will not abide :

THE WOMAN THAT WAS A SINNER.

You have your poor reward
   In *man's* approving look,
But His indignant wrath
   Such insult cannot brook."

" Proud host, to thy high guest
   No *water* gavest thou;
Thou gavest Him no *kiss*
   On pallid cheek or brow;
Not even *olive oil*
   Didst thou vouchsafe to shed,
In sweetly-soothing streams,
   Upon that holy head.

" But she, with gushing tears,
   Hath wash'd His wayworn feet;
And hath not ceas'd to press
   Fond kisses soft and sweet:
With those fair-flowing locks,
   Which grace her downcast head,
Those feet were fondly dried—
   With rarest ointment spread."

" Ye Pharisaic tribe,
   Who boast yourselves so clear
From sin's polluting stains,
   Look to your souls, and fear!

Ye feel no need of mercy,
  But *claim* a place above ;
And thus for Christ, your Saviour,
  How little is your love!

" But ye who, bow'd with sin,
  Have counted Jesus dear,
Ye in whose hearts the streams
  Of love run deep and clear,—
Look, penitents, to Heaven!
  The Saviour loveth such—
' To you much is forgiven,
  For you have lovèd much!' "

FLOWERS AND EARS OF CORN.

" Ye shall know them by their fruits."—Matt. vii. 16.

A fair young boy, in the fragrant breath
  Of a glowing Autumn morn,
Twin'd for himself a graceful wreath
  Of flowers and ears of corn.

FLOWERS AND EARS OF CORN.

Proudly he placed the fillet he made
   'Mid his waving golden hair,
And sported about o'er hill and glade
   With a happy, joyous air.

But soon the sun with its burning ray
   Pour'd down on the fair hill-side;
Till weary with heat, and tir'd of play,
   He cast the wreath aside.

The flow'rs soon lost their delicate bloom
   Beneath the scorching sun;
And soon they paled and wither'd away,
   And perish'd one by one:

But on the ears of corn, it seems,
   Its fierceness fell in vain;
For it only ripen'd them with its beams,
   And turn'd them into grain.

'Thus fade, thought I, the many vows,
   Array'd in seeming truth,
Which shine like flow'rs upon the brows
   Of gay and thoughtless youth:

FAITH.

They will not bear the scorching sun
    That tries them day by day;
But speedily wither, one by one,
    And die, and fall away.

But holy deeds, the fruits of faith,
    And done in Christian love—
These only ripen beneath the breath
    Of the sun which gleams above;

Till at last the joyful Harvest-home
    O'er earth's wide fields shall reign,
And troops of angel-reapers come
    To gather the golden grain.

FAITH.

(Impromptu.)

See yonder snowy bird, silently winging
    O'er the dark waters her joyous way!
Fearless she sleeps where their murmurs are ringing,
    And pillows her head 'mid the silvery spray.

Teach us thus, Lord, in this world of commotion—
    Daily deriving fresh courage from Thee—
Like the sea-bird which sports 'mid the roar of the ocean,
    As fearless, as trusting, as cheerful to be!

LIVING TEMPLES.

"Know ye not that ye are the temple of God; and that the Spirit of God dwelleth in you? If any man defile the temple of God, him shall God destroy; for the temple of God is holy, which temple ye are."—1 Cor. iii. 16, 17.

How fair, in page of Holy Writ,
    Judea's Temple stands!
'Twas God himself who fashion'd it
    By means of mortal hands:
'Twas He conceiv'd the grand design—
    The gates—the massive wall;
The outer courts—the inner shrine—
    The "Holiest of all."

Majestical it rose beneath
    The Master-builder's eye,
And soon, within its courts, the breath
    Of incense rose on high;
While priests, by altars stain'd with blood,
    Were loud in praise and pray'r,
And over all Shechinah stood
    To shew that God was there.

LIVING TEMPLES.

That temple charms no more the sight—
    Its stones are prostrate laid—
Its holy pomp, each solemn rite,
    Were doom'd of old to fade:
They were but *shadows* of the things
    Which Christians now possess—
The grey of early dawn which brings
    The Sun of Righteousness.

But God, our God, has Temples still,
    In which the faithful meet,
To hear their loving Master's will,
    And hymn His praises sweet.
'Tis there their spirits seem to leave
    This world for one above,
As they the pledges sweet receive
    Of Jesus' dying love.

And other Temples yet than these
    God has upon this earth;
'Tis only He, perchance, that sees
    Their unpretending worth.
They are not temples built of stone,
    Adorn'd by human skill;
But *hearts that worship Him alone,*
    And love to do His will.

LIVING TEMPLES.

In those still shrines some fav'rite sin
    Each day a victim dies;
And from those silent courts within
    Sweet pray'rs, like incense, rise.
There dwells a peace, which nought can mar,
    To soothe all earthly pains—
There, brighter than Shechinah far,
    God's blessed Spirit reigns!

That Spirit breathes upon the soul,
    And warms it into life;
'Tis ever present to control
    The evil that is rife;
It seals it as a child of grace,—
    As one of Jesus' band;
And gives an earnest of the bliss
    Of Heaven's promis'd land. ([1])

---

[1] Eph. i. 13., II Cor. i. 22.

DELIVER US FROM EVIL.

Matt. vi. 13.

In childhood's bright but fleeting years;
   In youth's fair Spring—in manhood's prime;
When tott'ring age itself appears,
   With locks all thin and hoar with time :—
Do thou, O God! when danger's rife,
   Thy gracious aid at once afford—
In ev'ry stage and path of life
   Deliver us from evil, Lord!

Where'er Thy will may bid us stray,
   On land, or on the changeful deep;
When 'neath the glorious light of day—
   When in thy care we sink to sleep;
When thieves the midnight silence break—
   When murd'rous fingers grasp the sword—
When Satan strives the soul to take—
   Deliver us from evil, Lord!

LOOK TO JESUS!

"Looking unto Jesus, the author (1) and finisher of our faith."—*Heb.* xii. 2.

Child of a lost and guilty race!
With dark, polluted, leprous soul;
An exile from thy Father's face,
Despising all his fond control,
Thy Saviour's hand can yet deface
Of sin's disease each ling'ring trace—
Oh! look to Jesus, and be whole!

Thou captive spirit! bound in chains,
Which Satan's hands have forg'd for thee;
Oh! shun the agonizing pains
Which wait thee in eternity.
From dungeon deep, where darkness reigns—
Look up to Heav'n! whilst hope remains,
Oh! look to Jesus, and be free!

---

(1) Marginal reading, *the beginner*.

LOOK TO JESUS.

Ye murm'ring mortals, bending low
    Beneath a load of human ill;
Though troubled waters round you flow,
    And bitter gall your cup may fill;
Though num'rous cares may now distress,
And none be nigh to aid and bless—
    Look, look to Jesus! Peace, be still!

Ye fainting pilgrims, as ye go
    This earth's sad wilderness along,
How oft will notes of deepest woe
    Be mingled in your wayside song!
Oft will your strength and vigour fail—
Oft will your very spirit quail—
    But look to Jesus, and be strong!

Departing saints, whom death doth call
    From earth and all its ties to sever;
Whatever clouds may round you fall
    Let faith and courage waver never!
Remember Jesus standeth by—
Soon shall ye meet his loving eye—
    Oh, look to Him, and live for ever!

THE CHRISTENING OF THE FIRST-BORN.

"For the promise is unto you, and to your children."—Acts ii. 39.

" Within God's sacred courts we bring
This day, our dearest earthly thing,—
A ' first-fruit off'ring ' to our King,
   In thee, our first-born, Marion !

" Thou art, sweet child, a blessing rare,
Committed to our tend'rest care ;
But One now claims a higher share,
   Than I, or mother, Marion !

" Thou art not only hers and mine ;
Thy baby brow now bears a sign,
Which makes thee Christ's and makes Christ thine,
   My little Christian Marion !

" Oh ! may the Spirit's quick'ning pow'r
Date thy ' new birth ' from this blest hour,
And train thee up a holy flow'r,
   To bloom in Heaven, Marion !

" I ask not for thee gems, nor gold,
Rare charms, broad lands, nor titles old ;
But safe within the Saviour's fold
   I'd have my little Marion.

THE CHRISTENING OF THE FIRST-BORN.

" There, in that ark, my gentle dove,
May'st thou behold that wondrous love
Which brought down Jesus from above,
  To save thee, happy Marion!

" Sweet charms will then thy spirit grace,
More fair than those of form or face,
And make thy heart a holy place
  For Christ to dwell in, Marion!

" Then should that Saviour summon thee
From earth and its delights to flee,
E'en in bright hours of infancy,—
  Thou'lt still be blest, my Marion!

" Or should He rather, one by one,
Bid father, mother, friends, begone,
And leave thee in this world alone,
  A little mourner, Marion!

" Still thou must meekly learn to bend
To Him from whom such blows descend,
And closer cling to that dear Friend
  Who'll never leave thee, Marion!

" ' I am Christ's, and Christ is mine,'
Oh, be this watchword ever thine!
A pillar of light and life divine
  For earth and Heav'n, my Marion!"

THE DEATH OF THE FIRST-BORN.

"I shall go to him, but he shall not return to me."—II Sam. xii. 23.

There was a tiny little *flow'r*
    That bloom'd beside our hearth;
It grew, 'mid sunshine and 'mid show'r,
    A lovely child of earth;
'Twas sweet to watch it day by day,—
    To view each op'ning grace,
And see the lights and shadows play
    Upon its winsome face.

There came a little rosy *beam*,
    And lighted up a home,
So bright and happy then, 'twould seem
    That sorrow could not come;—
A beam which from the aching heart
    Would ev'ry care beguile,
And bid the gath'ring clouds depart
    Before a joyous smile.

THE DEATH OF THE FIRST-BORN.

There was a little, silv'ry *voice*,
   So full of childish glee,
It seem'd to bid the world rejoice
   And make all sadness flee :
How softly on the summer air
   Its thrilling notes would rest !
And, oh, how sweet the echoes were
   It woke within the breast !

That *flow'r* has past from earth away,
   Its brief spring-tide is o'er ;
That rosy *beam* has ceas'd to play ;
   That *voice* is heard no more.
Its tender notes are hush'd and still
   Which bade our woes depart,
And never now can soothe or thrill
   The worn and weary heart.

But there's a bright, a blessed spot,
   Where things, for earth too pure,
Are dwelling now, without a blot
   Their glory to obscure ;
'Tis there that tender *flow'r* now blows,
   'Tis there that *beam* doth shine—
'Tis there that gentle *voice* now flows
   In harmonies divine !

THE DEATH OF THE FIRST-BORN.

We grieve to miss that little form—
    The *flow'r*, the *beam*, the *voice*—
Which prov'd our comfort in each storm,
    And made our hearts rejoice ;
But yet we are content to know
    That she is now at rest,
Beyond the pains of earth below,
    Upon her Saviour's breast.

We love to think upon her now,
    With Him who lov'd her so
That He must guard her infant brow
    From ev'ry line of woe ;
We love to think of that blest time,
    When we that home shall gain,
And in a brighter, happier clime,
    Embrace our child again.

"THY WILL BE DONE!"

Matt. vi. 10.

Jehovah! round Thy starry throne,
    All angels bow the knee;
Archangels know Thy will alone,
    And homage pay to Thee:
Then we, who are so little worth,
    Shall we obedience shun?
Like those in Heav'n, may we in earth,
    Exclaim " Thy will be done!"

When Hope deceives the trusting heart,
    And leaves it to despair;
When Fortune frowns, and friends depart,
    Too false our woe to share:
When sickness bids us leave the goal
    The toil of years hath won,—
Oh! teach us, still, with humbled soul,
    To say " Thy will be done!"

IN MEMORIAM.

When Sorrow makes the bosom smart,
   And bids the tear-drop flow;
When Death lets fly his ruthless dart,
   And lays some lov'd one low:
Whate'er our course through life may be—
   A calm or troubled one,—
Teach us, O Lord, to trust in Thee,
   And say "Thy will be done!"

IN MEMORIAM.

"Blessed are the pure in heart; for they shall see God."—*Matt.* v. 8.

Toll, toll a knell! sad tribute to the dead!
   Flow on uncheck'd, thou warmly-gushing tear!
Above the grave, One, more than human, shed
   Those precious drops, and all are human here.

How truly Mem'ry pictures to the mind
   That lovely form, expanding like the rose;
But chill'd and wither'd by th' unkindly wind,
   E'er she more ripen'd beauties could disclose!

IN MEMORIAM.

Dear to the heart the morn which hail'd her birth—
    The childish sports in which she play'd her part;
Her warm affection, and her deeds of worth—
    Her heav'nly mind—her purity of heart!

These—these are charms undimm'd by Death's dark frown,
    These—these are flow'rs whose beauty cannot die!
These shall entwine around her saintly crown,
    And bloom effulgent thro' Eternity!

How sadly, as each wak'ning sun arose,
    We mark'd that visage pale—that form grow weak!
And, as a fair day crimsons at its close,
    So lovelier grew the bloom upon her cheek:

Whilst that fair constellation of the heart—
    Sweet beaming Hope—dispell'd foreboding fear;
But soon its rays did one by one depart,
    We saw—we felt—Death's darksome hour draw near.

As o'er the mind float visions of the night,
    And leave us dazzled by the light they shed;
So purely, peacefully, serenely bright,
    Her seraph-spirit on its passage sped!

I WILL NOT LEAVE YOU COMFORTLESS.

Within the grave her mould'ring frame may rest,
And dew-drops sparkle on the verdant sod,
Yet shall she rise, in spotless garb be drest—
In brighter regions shall she " *see her God.*"

"I WILL NOT LEAVE YOU *COMFORTLESS*!" (1)

John xiv. 18.

Sweet words of comfort and of cheer
  For sorrow-stricken hearts,
When from its hidden source the tear
  Of bitter anguish starts;
When clouds of utter hopelessness
  Above us darkly low'r,
And through earth's dreary wilderness
  Blooms not a single flow'r!

Ye followers of Him whose head
  No earthly pillow press'd,
'Tis yours a rugged path to tread—
  Worn, weary, and distress'd;
And now that He, your Friend,—your Guide—
  Your Comforter—your *all*,—
Is soon to vanish from your side,
  Well may your spirits fall.

---

(1) Marginal reading, "*Orphans.*"

I WILL NOT LEAVE YOU COMFORTLESS.

Like children reft of father's care,
    Or watchful mother's love,
With none on earth those hopes to share
    Which lift your souls above ;
There shall be One beside you still
    Who never shall depart—
Oh ! let His tender accents thrill
    And animate your heart !

" I will not leave you comfortless ! "
    You shall not wander here,
Like *orphans*, with no sire to bless,
    To counsel or to cheer ;
He is your Friend,—your Father still,
    Unseen by mortal eye,
His spirit shall your bosom fill,
    And ev'ry need supply !

No bitter griefs your hearts can wring—
    No sin defile your soul—
But He can heal their bitter sting,
    And cleanse and make you whole ;
The mother may the babe forget, (1)
    Which smiles upon her breast—
His love shall ne'er grow dim nor set,
    But ever on you rest.

---

(1) Isaiah xlix. 15.

Fear not, disciples of the Lord!
  His Spirit cheers your way;
He can all grace and strength afford,
  However dark your day:
He leads you, by a path unknown,
  To bliss no tongue can tell,
Where anguish makes no bosom groan,
  And nought but joy can dwell.

ELEGY.

"I heard a voice from heaven saying unto me, Write, Blessed are the dead which die in the Lord from henceforth: yea, saith the Spirit, that they may rest from their labours; and their works do follow them."—*Rev.* xiv. 13.

Weep not for her, whose soul hath fled
  Beyond this new-rais'd tomb,
Where Sorrow's tears were freely shed,
  And Hope seem'd lost in gloom!
She is not dead—she is not here!
But risen to a happier sphere,
  Where joys eternal bloom.

ELEGY.

Weep not for her, whose blooming youth
    Disease hath worn away!
Rather rejoice she 'walked in truth,' (1)
    While yet 'twas early day;
And patiently and humbly trod
The narrow path that leads to God—
    That sweet, that holy way.

Weep not for her! for she is gone
    Where tears are never shed;
Where pain and trouble are not known—
    Where ev'ry care hath fled:
Array'd in snow-white raiment now—
A crown of glory on her brow—
    No! no! she is not dead!

Weep not for her! her work is done;
    The cross she meekly bore
Is laid aside, her race is run—
    Her holy strife is o'er:
Her soul at peace—her sins forgiv'n;
High-placed by Jesus' side in Heav'n—
    Mourner, what would'st thou more?

---

(1) III. Ep., John 4.

ELEGY.

Her's was the true, the sterling worth,
    That never knows decay,
Which can but shed, whilst yet on earth,
    A faint and dawning ray;
But, oh! when earth and earthly things
Have flown away on Time's swift wings,
    It blazes into day.

Weep not for her! could she declare
    The joys that round her reign,
You would not wish—you would not *dare*
    To call her back again:
Ear hath not heard, eye hath not seen
The glories of that blissful scene,— (1)
    Then let her there remain!

And, oh! remember, ye who love
    Her Heav'n-recorded name,
That faith which lifted her above,
    And firmly clasp the same;
Then, come what may of this world's care,
You yet shall meet in glory there,
    Beyond This earthly frame!

---

(1) Isaiah lxiv. 4., 1 Cor. ii. 9,

LIFE.

'Tis sweet to gaze on the broad expanse
    Of the deep and boundless ocean,
When the pale moon sheds its tranquil glance
    On its breast, devoid of motion:
When each sound is hush'd, and not a word
    By unhallow'd lip is spoken,
And even the sea-bird's cry 's unheard
    To intrude on the calm unbroken!

'Tis awful to see the dark waves roll—
    To list to their angry roaring,—
The thunder resounding from pole to pole,
    And the rain in torrents pouring:
To hear the spars snap, and the timbers creak,
    As they yield to the rushing billow,—
The mariner's last, despairing shriek,
    As he sinks to his watery pillow!

And such is life! now joy and peace—
    Now dark, distress'd, and troubled;
Till we reach that haven where storms shall cease,
    And all our joys be doubled.
Then, come! let us cast all fear aside,
    And hope and comfort borrow,
For there we may safely at anchor ride,
    Having past this sea of sorrow.

SUNSET REFLECTIONS.

"When it is evening, ye say, it will be fair weather: for the sky is red."
—*Matt.* xvi. 2.

Behold the fair Sun, as he sinks to his rest,
    In beauty and brilliancy glowing,
Gilding each ripple that plays on the breast
    Of the stream that is tranquilly flowing.

His bright course is run, he has gladden'd all hearts ;
    And to each child of nature hath given
Fresh strength, and he now, as he slowly departs,
    Sheds a promising glow over heaven.

As we gaze, let us pause, and consider the deeds
    Of the day, with a careful inspection ;
And, as from the mind each dark shadow recedes,
    Let it meet the keen eyes of Reflection.

Have we shunn'd what is ill ? have we lov'd what is right ?
    Have we lighten'd *one* heart of its sorrow ?
Has our conduct been such, should we perish this night,
    As to promise a blissful to-morrow ?

THINGS BELOVED.

"The works of the Lord are great, sought out of all them that have pleasure therein."—Psalm cxi. 2.

I love the calm and radiant sky—
    Those glowing orbs of light,
Which tread their silent path on high,
    And soften frowns of night:
I love each little lustrous star
    A Father's grace hath giv'n;
They seem like angels' eyes afar,
    To gaze from courts of heav'n.

I love vast ocean when it laves
    In peace the pebbly shore;
And when its high and crested waves
    Give out their giant roar:
I love the soft, mysterious sound,
    With which the streamlet flows;
'Tis like a pilgrim, heav'nward bound,
    A-singing as he goes.

THINGS BELOVED.

I love the fair and fragrant earth,
    Despite its gloom and care,
For noble deeds of honest worth,
    And faith and love are there;
I love the sunbeams 'mid its flow'rs—
    The strains of woodland choir;
The peace which reigns o'er Sabbath hours—
    The music of the spire.

I love fair childhood's beaming smile,
    Its ev'ry winning way;
I love to see it free from guile,
    And full of happy play:
But, oh! 'tis deck'd with *loveliest* charms,
    When, like the babes of old,
It smiles within the Saviour's arms—(1)
    A lamb of Jesus' fold.

I love God's sacred House of Prayer,
    Where kindred spirits meet
To bow with adoration there,
    And sit at Jesus' feet:
I love the high, and holy psalm—
    The evangelic hymn;
My soul they stimulate or calm,
    Like voice of Cherubim.

---
(1) Mark x. 15, 16.

THE FAMILY BIBLE.

But far above the dearest things
   On this attractive ball,
To Him my spirit fondly clings
   Who gave and blessed all :
To Him who, sinful man to free,
   Earth's wilds in sorrow trod—
To Him who made, and *sealeth me*, (¹)
   A happy child of God. (²)

THE FAMILY BIBLE.

"The law of thy mouth is better unto me than thousands of gold and silver. I will never forget thy precepts, for with them thou hast quickened me."—*Psalm* cxix. 72 and 93.

There is a venerable Book,
   On which my infant eyes
Would often gaze with mingled look
   Of rev'rence and surprise ;
Its very presence seem'd to change
   Or check youth's giddy stream,
Yet still it won—'twas passing strange !
   My young heart's high esteem.

---

(1) Ephes. i. 13, and iv. 30. (2) John i. 12, 13.

THE FAMILY BIBLE.

Each morn and eve, at hour of pray'r,
    Its holy light was pour'd
Within the silent chamber, where
    Its Author was ador'd;
And never on my father's face
    Did such sweet rapture dwell,
As when its words, so full of grace,
    From him in meekness fell.

I knew not then their meaning deep,
    But yet the voice was dear,
And oft I turn'd aside to weep,
    Or hide the gath'ring tear;
As, here and there, some tender truth
    Would thrill my thoughtless heart,
And even to the soul of youth
    Its quick'ning pow'r impart.

But soon that father's voice grew weak,—
    His aged eyes grew dim;
A pallor settled on his cheek—
    'Twas I then read to him:
And oh! though suff'ring tried without,
    And storms within grew rife,
How quickly fled each fear and doubt
    That vex'd his inner life!

THE FAMILY BIBLE.

His pale cheek wore a peaceful bloom,
    As, with Faith's purer sight,
He saw, beyond the yawning tomb,
    The saints' blest home in light.
Ah! yes, 'twas then I saw,—I *felt*
    Those truths to be divine,
And by that dying form I knelt,
    And pray'd they might be *mine*.

That Book is still my chosen friend —
    My comforter—my guide;
I'll trust it till life's latest end,
    Though all prove false beside:
For tho' its outward charms decay,
    I feel its *inward pow'r*
Grows stronger ev'ry passing day,
    And sweeter ev'ry hour:
Whilst often, as I sink to rest,
    I bless that father's tongue
Which sow'd '*the seed*' within my breast
    From which my peace has sprung.

INCENTIVES TO PRAISE.

"All thy works shall praise thee, O Lord; and thy saints shall bless thee."—*Psalm* cxlv. 10.

"Bless the Lord, O my soul, and forget not all his benefits."—*Psalm* ciii. 2.

Why do I praise Him? Go, ask yon flower,
   So fresh and so lovely in bloom,
Why it breathes on the air, from my gay little bower,
   Its fragrant and luscious perfume.

Why do I praise Him? Go, ask yon stream,
   Why it murmurs its grateful song,
As its bosom reflects the sun's fair beam,
   And it joyfully ripples along.

Why do I praise Him? Go, ask yon choir
   Why they warble their soul-thrilling lays
From the thicket, the brake, and the moss-cover'd spire,
   Thro' the long and serene summer days.

Each flower with fragrance and brightness of hue—
   Each stream with its murmuring sound—
Each bird with its song—tell their gratitude due
   To the Source whence all blessings abound.

A MOTHER'S HYMN.

And shall flowers, and streamlets, and birds of the air,
   Be full of God's glory and praise,
Whilst I, who His love more abundantly share,
   Not a strain of thanksgiving can raise?

Oh, no! 'tis He guides me,—He lightens my way;
   He aids me in every strife;
And therefore I praise Him by night and by day,
   And will till the close of my life.

A MOTHER'S HYMN.

"He shall give His angels charge over thee, to keep thee in all thy ways.
—*Psalm* xci. 11.

Gather, angels, gather round her;
   O'er her let thy wings be spread;
Let delightful dreams be found her,
   Scatter blessings o'er her head.

Warble, angels, warble o'er her,
   Tender strains of joy and peace;
Smooth the path that lies before her,
   Bid all sin's delusions cease.

BOCHIM.

Guard her, angels, whilst reposing,
   Keeping loving watch and true;
Let those eyes, like violets closing,
   Open to the morning dew.

Guard that body—fairer flower
   Ne'er to deck this earth was giv'n;
Keep it from each driving shower,
   Warm it with the beams of heav'n.

Guard that soul—that priceless treasure,
   And, should that form no more arise,
Bear it to scenes of holy pleasure,—
   Endless bliss beyond the skies.

BOCHIM. [1]

"And it came to pass, when the angel of the Lord spake these words unto all the children of Israel, that the people lifted up their voice, and wept. And they called the name of that place Bochim."—Judges ii. 4, 5.

Through Bochim's valley all must tread,—
   Some bitter, burning tears,
Must ev'ry heav'n-bound pilgrim shed,
   Before his home appears:

---

[1] "Weepers"; "place of weeping."

BOCHIM.

Before he sees his Father's face,
    In realms of endless day;
Before in Jesus' fond embrace,
    All tears are wiped away.

Dark deeds of sin, wrought long ago,
    In wild and thoughtless youth,
Whilst yet we wander'd to and fro,
    Strangers to God and truth,—

These oft, like ghosts, will leave the tomb,
    In stillness of the night,
Oppress the heart with deepest gloom,
    The trembling soul affright:

Many the dreary, sleepless nights,—
    Many the tears and prayers,
Before these grim and ghastly sprites
    Are driven from their lairs!

Beside some little grassy mound,
    With clinging wild-flow'rs drest,
Oft will some kneeling form be found,
    By 'whelming grief opprest:

BOCHIM.

Some must, like kingly David, weep
    Above a sickly child: (1)
Some must, like faithful Rizpah, keep
    Death-watch on mountain wild: (2)

Some o'er their own deep-seated woes,
    The flowing tears must shed;
Whilst others, Christ-like, weep o'er those,
    Whose day of grace is fled.

The easily besetting sin—
    The secret, gnawing woe—
These wring the grieving soul within,
    And make the sad drops flow:

These drive us to the 'sinner's Friend,'
    These lift our thoughts above;
In Him our dark forebodings end,—
    There grief is lost in love.

---

(1) II *Sam.* xii. 22.
(2) II *Sam.* xxi. 10.

NO MORE DEATH.

(Rev. xxi. 4.)

There is a pallid spectre, (¹)
    With swift but silent tread,
O'er earth for ever moving,
    And filling all with dread:

His person no man knoweth,
    His form is never seen;
But tears and groans of anguish
    Proclaim where he hath been.

He climbs the park-girt palace,
    Where monarchs dwell in state;
Passes the marble portal—
    The sentry at the gate;

And, lo! a prince lies sleeping
    Beneath his crimson pall,
Whilst sadly tears are falling
    In hamlet and in hall.

---

(1) "Pallida Mors æquo pulsat pede pauperum tabernas Regumque turres."—Hor. Lib. I. 4.

NO MORE DEATH.

Through cottage porch he enters,
  Where wreathing creepers cling,—
Where, 'mid the merry sunshine,
  The birds all gaily sing:

There Nature's sweetest incense
  Is breathed upon the gale,
But, in a darken'd chamber,
  There lies an infant pale.

Oh, flow'rs may bud and blossom,
  The jasmine perfume fling,—
The stream may murmur softly,
  The wild-birds sweetly sing:

Their charms can never solace
  The grieving spirit's pain;
Their voices cannot waken
  That form to life again;

But some fond Rachel, weeping,
  Must rend the startled air;— (1)
O Death! hast thou no pity,
  That thou could'st enter there?

---

(1) *Matt.* ii. 18. *Jer.* xxxi. 15.

NO MORE DEATH.

Thus over earth's dark surface,
    And o'er the boundless main,
Glides on that noiseless spectre,
    Tears ever in his train;

And daily some new tomb-stone,
    Or little grassy mound,—
Some gurgling of the water,
    Or dull and plashing sound,—

Proclaims another mortal
    Gone to his latest rest,
Beneath earth's sparkling dew-drops,
    Or ocean's heaving breast.

Oh, for that blessed season
    When saints shall rise again,
To share a glorious kingdom,
    Where Death shall never reign!

Oh, for that happy region
    Beyond his blighting breath,—
Those bright and blissful mansions,
    Where shall be "no more death!"

THE ÆOLIAN HARP.

"The wind bloweth where it listeth, and thou hearest the sound thereof, but canst not tell whence it cometh, and whither it goeth: so is every one that is born of the Spirit."—*John* iii. 8.

I placed a sweet Æolian lyre
   My open window near;
No music flow'd at my desire,
   Until a zephyr dear
Breath'd softly on each tuneful string,
And made their sweet-ton'd voices ring
   Upon the list'ning ear.

My soul was silent—bound in sin,
   Till God's sweet Spirit came
Its dark and desert shrines within,
   To wake, to thrill, to tame:
Now happy music soundeth there,—
The music of believing prayer,
   Pour'd forth in Jesus' name.

THE COMING YEAR.

Oh, would that every spell-bound soul
    Would crave that Spirit's breath,
To free from Satan's dark control,
    And silence deep as death!
Then, breathing forth their notes divine,
Earth would become one holy shrine,
    The dome of Heav'n beneath.

Alas! that tuneless chords should jar
    'Mid that sweet melody!
Born from above, (1) sin yet doth mar
    Our converse with the sky:
But soon the hand of boundless Love
Shall each discordant string remove,
    Till all is harmony.

---

(1) *John.* iii. 3. (Marginal reading "from above.")

THE COMING YEAR.

"My days are swifter than a weaver's shuttle."—Job vii. 6.
"So teach us to number our days, that we may apply our hearts unto wisdom."—Psalm xc. 12.

Another year has glided o'er,
   Of mingled bliss and sorrow;
Its beams and clouds return no more
   To gild or shroud the morrow.
'Tis gone! 'tis gone beyond recall!
   Like nightly vision, vanish'd;
Soon will its ling'ring traces all,
   By fresher scenes be banish'd.

Fair flow'rs will wreathe the new-raised tomb
   Where some lov'd form is sleeping,
And solace with their fragrant bloom
   The hearts now sore with weeping:
Array'd in smiles will be the cheek
   Where Sorrow's rills are streaming;
Whilst eyes, which deepest woe bespeak,
   Will soon with joy be beaming.

THE COMING YEAR.

Once more, o'er all the verdant plain,
    Throughout Earth's fragrant bowers,
Will Spring resume her transient reign,
    And ope the budding flowers;
Fair types of human hopes, whose smile
    Deluded bosoms cherish,—
Ah! doom'd, like them, to bloom awhile,
    And then to fade and perish.

Next, Summer will display the charms,
    As time is onward creeping;
And Autumn bare her sunburnt arms,
    To gather in her reaping,
Ere Winter comes with hurrying feet
    To veil the wreck of nature,
And, with her snowy winding-sheet,
    To shroud each wither'd feature.

Those anxious aims for fame and gain,
    But form'd to be defeated;
That chequer'd round of varied pain,
    Again will be repeated,
Until, released, our heads have press'd
    The dreamless death-bed pillow,
Like weary sea-birds sunk to rest
    On life's expended billow.

SEED-TIME.

The warrior's pride—the statesman's care—
    Each sigh for pomp or pow'r,
Will wake no answering echo there,
    In that calm, peaceful hour;
But each bright deed of faith and love,
    Their holy radiance blending,
Will crown the saint, to realms above
    On angel-wings ascending.

SEED-TIME.

"In the morning sow thy seed; and in the evening withhold not thine hand."—*Eccles.* xi. 6.

"Blessed are ye that sow beside all waters."—*Isaiah* xxxii. 20.

Life is thy seed-time, brother man,
    The soil is ready and meet;
The time before thee is but a span,
    But the furrows are under thy feet.
Freely did'st thou of thy Lord receive,
    Mercy, and pity, and love;
Freely, then, of thy fulness give, ([1])
    Sow now, and reap above!

---

(1) 1 Matt. x. 8.

SEED-TIME.

Gaze on those shivering sons of want,
    Hungry, and chill, and bare,
With famish'd eyes, with clothing scant,
    And wild, neglected air:
Here scatter thy seed and it shall bring
    Fruit to a hundred-fold;
From deserts as barren as this shall spring
    More than thy barns can hold.

See yon pale mother tending her charge,
    With faded and care-worn cheek;
Slender her means, her family large,
    Her husband ailing and weak;
She will not stoop to the beggar's trade,
    But work on till she drop—
A few seeds here of kindly aid,
    Will yield thee a noble crop.

A felon lies in yon darken'd cell,
    Brooding in silence grim;
To-morrow will ring his dying knell,
    Hast thou no seed for him?
Not a pitying tear? not a word of hope?
    Not an interceding pray'r?
Before the grip of the strangling rope
    Launches his spirit—*where?*

SEED-TIME.

Go, Christian sower—go bravely forth!
    Be *love* thy precious seed;
Go East and West! go South and North!
    For pressing is the need;
There are wounded spirits and hopeless breasts,
    And cheeks ne'er free from tears;
There are minds where ignorance deeply rests,
    Together with slavish fears:
Where'er thou turnest thy wand'ring feet,
    Through this sad world below,
There is plenty of soil ready and meet
    For that thou hast to sow.

Sow not thro' a love of this world's pelf,
    Nor for *man's* approving nod;
Sow not through a paltry love of self,
    But sow through a *love to God!*
See, too, Brother, thy seed be cast
    Not with a niggardly hand,
That thou may'st reap, when thy toils are past,
    On the plains of the promis'd land.

SEASONS OF PRAYER.

"Evening, and morning, and at noon, will I pray, and cry aloud ; and He shall hear my voice."—Psalm lv. 17.

Bright beams the blushing morn,
    The night has flown away ;
Fair flow'rs the fields adorn,
    The sunbeams brightly play ;
The lark's song sweet and clear,
    Rings through the balmy air ;
Now, meekly drawing near,
    How sweet the hour of pray'r!

'Tis noon ! the drooping flowers
    Look faint—the brook is dry ;
The sun's exhausting powers
    The face of Nature try ;
To yonder river's brink
    The thirsting flocks repair :
So, when thy spirits sink,
    Go, seek thy God in pray'r!

UNDER THE SNOW.

'Tis ev'ning's holy hour!
   All Nature whispers peace;
Closed is each dewy flow'r—
   The world's loud murmurs cease;
Now, in this calm so sweet,
   When all around is fair,
Bow low at Jesus' feet,
   Pour forth thy soul in pray'r!

Thus in the morn of life,
   And at its noon, and eve,
Whatever storms be rife,—
   Whatever make thee grieve,—
Oft steal from earth away,
   Its sorrow and its care,
And let each passing day
   Be sanctified by prayer.

UNDER THE SNOW.*

"Thou shalt quicken me again, and shalt bring me up again from the depths of the earth!"—Psalm lxxi. 20.

Under the snow—four foot low—
   I laid a child to rest;
Her form was chill, her lips were still—
   No pulse within her breast:
In her eye no light, and her brow as white
   As the flow'rs her fingers press'd.

Under the snow—four foot low—
   That tiny form was laid;
The feeble ray of a winter day,
   Above her lightly play'd;
And a little mound of frozen ground
   Was all the tribute paid.

---

* The first child the author was called upon to inter, after the decease of his own little one, was buried in the winter of the year 1860, remarkable for its heavy falls of snow: the two circumstances became insensibly blended in his mind, as he wrote the following verses.

UNDER THE SNOW.

Under the snow—four foot low—
    I left that sleeping child;
But Spring came round, with merry sound,
    And the air was fresh and mild;
The grass waved green, where the snow had been,—
    And birds sang sweet and wild:

Still, under the snow—cold and low—
    She lies in my memory;
For no *earthly* Spring can ever bring
    My darling back to me:
I ne'er can hear that voice so dear—
    That light step bounding free!

Thus, under the snow,—four foot low—
    That form still silent lies;
But a Spring shall shine, and a voice divine
    Shall one day bid it rise;
So I will not weep, for the angels keep
    That grave in their loving eyes.

When earth and its snow, beneath the glow
    Of that spring, shall melt away,
That form shall rise beyond the skies,
    And bask in Heaven's ray,—
Shall re-unite with the spirit bright,
    Which left it lifeless clay.

"IN THE TROUGH OF THE SEA."*

"Out of the depths have I cried unto thee, O Lord."—Psalm cxxx. i.

Days and nights in the '*trough of the sea,*'
    A great ship, lab'ring, lay;
Suns rose and set on the waves, but she
    Rode not upon her way;
Whilst the shadowy wings of Eternity
    Brooded from day to day.

As stormy waves did round her leap,
    What sights, what sounds were there!
Low-muttered curses many and deep—
    Dark looks of wild despair;
With pallid faces, e'en in sleep,
    Beaming with peace and pray'r.

---

* Suggested by the disaster which befel the giant steamship, 'The Great Eastern,' in the month of September, A.D. 1861.

"IN THE TROUGH OF THE SEA."

Days and nights in the '*trough of the sea*,'
   Exposed to Ocean's rage,
Sunk in a state of misery,
   Which naught could then assuage,
Each long day seem'd like a century—
   Each gloomy night an age.

Days and nights in the '*trough of the sea*,'
   My spirit, lab'ring, lay;
Heav'n seem'd to have no smile for me,
   And Hope no kindly ray;
Wounded and bruis'd, I could not see
   A step of the onward way.

The troubled waters rose and roar'd,
   Clouds veiled the radiant sky;
Where once its cheering light was pour'd
   I met Despair's dull eye;
But I cried to Thee, my gracious Lord!
   And Thou did'st hear my cry.

Thy loving smile the darkness broke,
   Thy grace renew'd my might,
And soon my spell-bound spirit woke
   Beneath its cheering light;
And now I stem, with a bolder stroke,
   The billows, foaming white.

"IN THE TROUGH OF THE SEA."

I see my weakness, O my God!
 I see Thy might divine;
I love the hand that grasps the rod—
 The face that would not shine;
And I worship Him who the billows trod,
 For the peace which now is mine.

I praise Thee, Lord, for every smile
 Thou deemest good for me;
Yes, and for every proving trial,
 Which draws me nigh to Thee :
For I know Thou lov'dst me even while,
 I lay in '*the trough of the sea*'!

"BEAR YE ONE ANOTHER'S BURDENS."

Gal. vi. 2.

'Bear ye one another's burdens,'
   Pilgrim-saints for Zion bound!
Seek and crave no other guerdons,
   But what in Jesus' smiles are found.

When some bruised and fallen brother
   Drops upon the world's highway,
Though scorn'd and left by ev'ry other,
   Turn not ye your eyes away.

Let false, self-righteous worldlings cherish,
   Coldness, selfishness and pride;
Leave not ye a soul to perish—
   Pass not on the other side! [1]

But, like Him, the loving Jesus—
   Who cares for all that breathe below,
And who from every sorrow frees us—
   Look kindly on a brother's woe.

Dispel his spirit's sinful blindness,
   Soothe its wounds with oil and wine;
Speak to him with words of kindness—
   Speak to him of grace divine.

---

[1] *Luke* x. 30.

"BEAR YE ONE ANOTHER'S BURDENS."

Pity his forlorn condition ;
    Comfort, counsel, warn, entreat ;
Let it be your blessed mission
    To lead him to the Saviour's feet.

Shun not homes though poor and lowly,
    There true riches oft are stor'd ;
Yet, however blest and holy,
    Its inmates need a kindly word.

Poverty has many trials,
    Often unbefriended stands ;
How welcome, 'mid its self-denials,
    Feeling hearts and helping hands !

Fly not spots where earthly sorrow—
    Where care and pining sickness reign ;
There sad or sick from thee may borrow
    Balm to soothe their bitter pain.

Fly not scenes where deathless spirits
    Leave their prison-house of clay
For realms in which the saint inherits
    Glory that shall ne'er decay:

"BEAR YE ONE ANOTHER'S BURDENS."

Where restless heads press dying pillows,
    Dew'd with penitential tears;
Until, above sin's 'whelming billows,
    Jesus' loving form appears.

Shun not, then, these daily meetings
    With poverty, disease, and death;
These are times when friendly greetings
    Come like Spring's reviving breath.

Oh, 'tis then words fitly spoken
    Pierce the souls of those that roam,
And, when the cords of sin are broken,
    Lead repentant wand'rers home.

"Bear ye one another's burdens,"
    As this world ye travel thro';
Seek not perishable guerdons—
    Bear, *because He bore for you!*

Cares and troubles shar'd with others,—
    Sorrows cheer'd with Christian love,
Make a commonwealth of brothers,
    Such as dwell with Christ above.

MY CHURCH.

"How dreadful is this place! this is none other but the house of God, and this is the gate of Heaven."—Gen. xxviii. 17.

There is a spacious fane uprear'd
   In honour of the Lord,
Where He is pleased to summon me
   To preach His gracious word:
To wear an ephod, and to lead
   Those notes of praise and pray'r,
Which He himself vouchsafes to heed
   From realms of upper air.

No architectural beauties grace
   Its unpretending aisles,
No sculpture such as finds a place
   In grand cathedral piles;
No painted windows tint each ray
   That plays athwart the floor,
No high-carv'd cherubim display
   Their wings above the door.

MY CHURCH.

And yet I know it has its charms
    In its good Master's eyes,
And trust it gathers in its arms,
    Blest souls for yonder skies :
Oh! may it prove like dews of even
    To spirits worn and faint—
A happy, long-sought gate of Heaven,
    To many a weary saint!

There, blessed Lord, we wait on Thee,
    When Sabbath mornings rise ;
There craving spirits look to me,
    With earnest, yearning eyes :
Full oft I tremble as I stand
    Within those sacred walls—
The sight of that assembled band
    My very soul appals.

How shall I charge these, face to face,
    To shun each hateful sin?
When *I* still have so little grace—
    So much of guilt within :
Whilst in the wilderness I stray,
    With faint and wavering tread,
How shall I lead these on the way?
    How fill these souls with bread?

My Saviour! I will look to thee—
Thou wilt my need supply;
None e'er can weak or empty be
When Thou art standing by:
From Thee will I, beloved Lord!
The bread of life receive— ([1])
Low at thy feet, first hear the Word,
Then to thy people give.

SMILES AND TEARS.

" To every thing there is a season, and a time to every purpose under the heaven. A time to weep, and a time to laugh; a time to mourn and a time to dance."—*Eccles.* iii. 1, 4.

Laugh when the skies are warm and bright;
When the mind is free and the heart is light;
When not a cloud looms on the sight;—
   Laugh! Laugh!

Weep when the bloom of life hath fled;
When the last sear leaf of hope is shed;
When the cherished friends of youth lie dead;—
   Weep! Weep!

(1) Matt. xv. 36.

"HEART TREASURES."

Laugh when the joys of life are green;
Weep when the pangs of grief are keen;
Laugh and weep thro' the chequer'd scene;—
          Laugh and weep!

Laughing and weeping, must we go
O'er the changeful face of earth below;
Till the sunshine of Heav'n around us glow,
          Where none can weep!

"HEART TREASURES."

"There is treasure to be desired, and oil, in the dwelling of the wise."—Prov. xxi. 20.

"The law of thy mouth is better unto me than thousands of gold and silver."—Psalm cxix. 72.

I would not yield these hopes of mine—
    The peace this heart hath known,
For all the wealth and pomp that shine
    Around a monarch's throne;
More sweetly they my griefs beguile,
    And cheer my dreary way,
Than Pleasure's soft ensnaring smile,
    Or proud Ambition's ray.

"HEART TREASURES."

The regal crown may grace a brow
    That aches with inward care;
Rare gems may gleam on breasts of snow,
    Dark temples of Despair;
The beams of Pleasure shine awhile,
    But only to betray;
And who would seek Ambition's smile
    For triumphs of a day?

But hopes that lift the soul above—
    Sweet peace within the heart—
The tokens of a Saviour's love—
    These never can depart:
The gloomier the path we tread,
    The sweeter is their pow'r;
And, oh, how bright the beams they shed
    On life's last solemn hour!

THE PROTO-MARTYR.

"And they stoned Stephen, calling upon God, and saying, Lord Jesus receive my spirit."—Acts vii. 59.

Bleeding and crushed the martyr lies
    The frowning rock beneath,
With face upturn'd to yonder skies,
    And still, suspended breath;
But peace and joy are with him now,
The light of Heaven gleams on his brow,
    All damp with dews of death.

Stern eyes glare on that mangled form—
    Fierce shouts rise on the air;
He heedeth not the angry storm
    Which rages round him there:
He sees the throng—the angel-throng;
His ears are full of holy song—
    His soul is full of pray'r!

Softly his spirit soars away,
    And wings its flight on high;
He sinks upon his couch of clay,
    'Mid this rude lullaby,

THE PROTO-MARTYR.

Wrapt in a sleep as sweet and mild
As e'er he slumber'd, when a child,
    Beneath his mother's eye. (1)

To early tomb that corpse is borne—
    With loving kindness drest;
Whilst many a Christian friend, forlorn,
    Weeps sadly on his breast; (2)
Yes, many are the tear-drops shed,
And softly is the dark earth spread
    Above his place of rest.

First on the bright, but crimson page
    Of martyr'd men of God,
Who, slain for Christ, in every age
    Have cried from earth's dark sod!
Many another, faint and worn,
Mangled and crushed, defaced and torn,
    Must tread where thou hast trod.

When earth's sharp trials fall thick on me,
    And break my spirit down,
God give me grace to think of thee,
    And dare the world's dark frown!
God grant me steadfast to abide,
That I may worship at thy side,
    And wear the saintly crown!

(1) Acts vii. 60.
(2) Acts viii. 2.

LIGHT IN DARKNESS.*

"When I sit in darkness, the Lord shall be a light unto me."—*Micah* vii. 8.

Father, you cannot bear to see
    These dim and sightless eyes;
It pains you when you think of me—
    The gloom that on me lies:

I bless you for your loving care,
    Your words and accents kind;
But banish doubt and dark despair,
    Mourn not that I am blind.

'Tis true I cannot see the mild,
    Bright sun that glows above—
The grove I play'd in when a child—
    The flow'rs I used to love:

---

* These verses were suggested by several most interesting interviews which the Author held with a member of his flock, who had been afflicted with blindness; they by no means exaggerate the spiritual and more than resigned tone of her mind.

LIGHT IN DARKNESS.

'Tis true these eyes will ne'er again
   Behold the babbling brook—
The wild vine 'cross the window-pane—
   My fav'rite garden nook.

A settled darkness hides from me
   The old familiar room,
In which I grew from infancy
   To happy girlhood's bloom :

But all my spirit held most dear
   Is stamp'd upon my mind,
So deep, so vivid, and so clear,
   I cannot deem me blind!

To me the flow'rs are ever fair,
   Those beams have never paled ;
Your faces are as free from care,
   As when my sight was veil'd :

'Tis merciful it should be so!
   'Twould pain me could I see
The traces of your silent woe,
   Or anxious fears for me.

LIGHT IN DARKNESS.

Though gloom my outward vision shrouds,
   A clear and *inward* light
Has scatter'd all the murky clouds,
   Which dimm'd my *spirit's* sight:

I see myself,—I see my God,
   So plainly, clearly now,
I can but *bless* the chast'ning rod
   Which makes me meekly bow.

I see—I see my fearful guilt,
   As ne'er I saw before;
My scorn for blood by Jesus spilt—
   For all the pangs he bore:

I see my vanity and pride,
   My cold and selfish ways;
His mercy leaves no cloud to hide
   These from my quicken'd gaze.

But whilst I thus with tears behold
   This stain'd, polluted soul,
And see the bitter Past unfold
   Its dark and blotted scroll:

LIGHT IN DARKNESS.

Although an erring child, I see
    In God a Father kind,
Who yearns to save and welcome me,—
    Oh, no, I am not blind!

I know that I have Jesus' love—
    His pardon for my sin;
He whispers me of bliss above,
    He gives me peace within.

No words of mine can e'er declare
    What joys surround me now,—
But can you mark one shade of care
    Upon this happy brow?

Fear not, my father dear, for me,
    A dark world doom'd to tread,
You see not what your child can see
    Of brightness over-head:

Believe that He who turns my night
    To fair and peaceful day,
Will ever keep me in His sight,
    Nor let His blind one stray.

UNITED PRAYER.

Grieve not, then, o'er thy sightless child,
    Restrain thy flowing tears ;
Hers is a lot by heaven beguil'd,
    And void of earthly fears :

But weep for those who, having eyes,
    See not the things of God ;
Who leave the pathway to the skies,
    Neglected and untrod !

UNITED PRAYER.

"They lifted up their voice to God with one accord. *And when they had prayed, the place was shaken where they were assembled together; and they were all filled with the Holy Ghost."—Acts iv. 24, 31.*

If he whom music doth inspire,
Touch but *one* string of tuneful lyre,
How doth its tender tribute greet
The list'ning ear with music sweet !
Whilst each vibration seems to thrill
The eager soul, and gently still,
With accents soft, the waves of care
Which roll'd their 'whelming waters there :

UNITED PRAYER.

But when his skilful hand he flings
Across a *multitude* of strings,
And all their tuneful notes *combine*,
Then, oh, what harmony divine !
How doth it stir the silent deep
Where all our tend'rest feelings sleep,—
Bid springs gush forth then first unseal'd,
And sympathies ne'er yet reveal'd,
Which shed their influence on the soul,
And bid us weep beyond control ;
Till on the tide of gushing tears
A thousand dark and anxious fears,
With yearnings, not unmix'd with pain,
Are swept away,—and joy doth reign !

'Tis thus, when God's blest Spirit breaks
Upon a sin-bound soul, and wakes
The music of believing pray'r,
The Father bends from upper air !
Those broken accents, new desires,
A sense of sinfulness inspires ;
Those rapt, ecstatic words which tell
Of joys ineffable that swell
The bosom of the child of God,
Who by the Saviour's side hath trod,
Each individual note of pray'r
Wakes a responsive rapture there,

UNITED PRAYER.

As He, with yearning heart doth bound
To clasp a child, once lost, now found :
Or as He sees, with tender thrill,
One, long beloved, draw nearer still.

But if our God doth deem so sweet,
Those spirit utt'rances which greet
His loving ear from *one* full soul,
When freed from sin's accurs'd control,
How must He long and love to hear
When goodly *multitudes* draw near,
And, with one voice and one accord,
Pour forth their wants before their Lord !
Beseeching, with *united* cry,
Rich blessings from His throne on high.
He leans towards that kneeling throng,
Their burden, dear as angels' song,
Pierces the gloomy pall of Night,
Climbs swiftly up the starry height,
Enters ' *the holiest* ' above,
And wakens all a Father's love.

May all the Church, in union sweet,
Thus oft before Jehovah meet ;
Not merely from her altars *lone*,
May she with pray'rs besiege His throne :

UNITED PRAYER.

But at *one common altar* raise
Such 'hecatombs' of pray'r and praise,
As shall bid Satan turn and flee,
And fill all Heav'n with minstrelsy!

Oh! ere that savor yet can rise
Beyond the over-arching skies,—
Before those words can reach His ear,
That gracious God will haste to hear;
Will 'rend the heavens and come down,'
His Church with lasting glory crown;
Will ne'er permit her light to fail,
Nor let the gates of hell prevail:
Will bind around her radiant brow
Wreaths that shall bloom resplendent now,
But lovelier glow in that pure clime,
Where blighting sin and with'ring Time
No more can injure or defile,
Or rob her of the Bridegroom's smile.

SPIRITUAL LONGINGS.

'We that are in this tabernacle do groan, being burdened: not for that we would be unclothed, but clothed upon, that mortality might be swallowed up of life."—2 Cor. v. 4.

When shall I see my Saviour king,
 On His all-glorious throne,
And hear the bright-wing'd angels sing
 Sweet songs, on earth unknown?
When shall I see the white-rob'd saints,
 Before him, radiant, stand,
A crown on ev'ry beaming brow,
 A palm in ev'ry hand?
When shall I see that Father's face,
 So yearn'd for, and so dear?
When shall I once again embrace
 The friends who cheer'd me here?

Be still, my longing soul! Be still!
 Await the solemn hour
When He, who governs all at will,
 Shall speak to thee in pow'r;

SPIRITUAL LONGINGS.

Shall burst the chains that bind to earth,
    And bid thee soar away
To that blest home of thy new birth,
    Where shines eternal day.
Be still, my longing soul! Be still!
    Be watchful unto pray'r!
Bow meekly to thy Saviour's will,
    And thou shalt see him there.

Thine ears shall catch such strains as thrill
    No earth-bound souls below;
Such joys thy yearning heart shall fill,
    As mortals cannot know:
The strains of Heav'n, so sweet—so clear,
    Its scenes so dazzling bright,—
These are too high for *earthly* ear,
    Too pure for earthly sight!
But when thou art by Jesus' side,
    Array'd in living light,
Then, longing soul, how full the tide
    Of exquisite delight!

DAYS THAT ARE GONE.

" My days are swifter than a post: they flee away, they see no good. They are passed away as the swift ships: as the eagle that hasteth to the prey."— Job ix. 25, 26.

Why should ye mourn o'er the days that are gone?
    Look hopefully on to the morrow:
Tears must flow on till existence is done,
    For Earth is a temple of Sorrow!

Why should ye mourn o'er the days that are gone,
    Who in beauty and youth are declining?
'Tis the hand of your Father that beckons you on,
    His love o'er your pathway is shining!

Why should ye mourn o'er the days that are gone,
    Whose heads are o'er-silver'd with age?
Wish not o'er life's volume to linger so long,—
    To pause o'er its last dreary page!

Why should ye mourn o'er the days that are gone,
    Whose hearts pain and anguish have riven?
There's a balm that will soothe, there's a bliss to atone,
    There's a peace that's unbroken in Heaven!

THE OLD MAN'S GOD.

Why should ye mourn o'er the days that are gone,
    Who in Piety's footsteps have trod ?
Each day, o'er thy head as it swiftly hath flown,
    Hath brought thee more near to thy God!

Then mourn not o'er days that are vanish'd and gone,
    Though they fair and unclouded were given,
The brightest of beams that on earth ever shone
    Is gloom to the glory of Heaven.

THE OLD MAN'S GOD.

"Even to your old age I am he; and even to hoar hairs will I carry you.—*Isai.* xlvi. 4.

I am weary and old, and wither'd and grey ;
My sap and vigor have pass'd away ;
I stand, like a leafless, desolate tree ;
For the world has no need, no thought of me.
But there was a time, when supple and strong,
I rose with the sun, and my cheery song
The silence deep of the forest broke,
As the tall trees fell at my sturdy stroke.

THE OLD MAN'S GOD.

There was a time when I ask'd no aid
To earn my own and my children's bread;
When I almost scorn'd the agèd and weak,
As I granted the boon they came to seek:
But, alas! I have lived long enough to see
That increasing years bring infirmity;
I have felt in my turn that the world is cold,
And cares little or naught for the feeble and old.

The hands that have cut the forest down,
Oft reap not the sheaves which the *clearing* crown;
The eyes that have watch'd the clicking loom,
From the grey of dawn to the evening's gloom,
Oft look in vain for their daily bread,
And a pillow to rest a hoary head;
For them the toil, and the failing health,
For another the pleasure and pomp of wealth.

As long as the body can slave away,
There is plenty of toil and a trifle of pay;
But when the vigor of life is sped,
Who cares where the *pauper* gets his bread?
He may live on the road and lie in a ditch,
His withered old wife may starve or stitch;
The labour of years has broken his back,
And who heeds what becomes of a worn out hack?

THE OLD MAN'S GOD.

O God! I had lain me down and died,
Years, years ago, by the lone wayside;
I had lain me down in sheer despair,
Were it not that I felt that *Thou wert there;*
Were it not for the comfort and peace I found
In Thee, when the skies were dark around;
Were it not for the hopes which fill'd my breast
Of the home where the weary may find a rest.

I bow'd at Thy feet, with a heart defiled
With a thousand sins, but thou hast smiled
By night and by day on my lonely way,
And kindlier still as my locks grew grey.
Then, what is the scorn of the world to me?
What are its gloom, and its penury?
When I can look up, from a couch on the sod,
With faith and hope, to *the old man's God*.

ON TO GLORY!

"I reckon that the sufferings of this present time are not worthy to be compared with the glory which shall be revealed in us."—*Rom.* viii. 18.

On to glory! On to glory!
Not where battle-fields are gory,
   And heaps of slain defile the ground;
Not where forms in death are sleeping—
Not where broken hearts are weeping,
   And greedy vultures hover round.

On to glory! On to glory!
Where Heav'n's high records tell the story,
   Where angel-hands the victor crown;
Where the hosts of Hell are flying,
Where Death himself is now a dying,
   And Satan's hurl'd to darkness down.

On to glory! On to glory!
Where time has waxen old and hoary,
   And sunk with Earth into decay;
But where the honor which is given
By Jesus to his saints in Heaven,
   Beams more resplendent day by day.

HOMEWARD BOUND.

"He bringeth them unto their desired haven."—Psalm cvii. 30.

' Homeward bound! Homeward bound!'
    Hark to the thrilling cry!
The joyful sound fast spreads around,
    And rends the lofty sky:
The roughest seaman 'mid us found
    Has not an eyelid dry.

The brave ship's weather'd many a gale,
    And many a raging sea,
When the fierce blasts rent her swelling sail
    And curb'd her spirit free,
'Mid foaming reefs, where cheeks grew pale
    At thought of Eternity.

But now the storms are all forgot,
    And Ocean's angry foam,
Has only endeared the native spot
    To the hearts of those that roam;
Glad dreams now brighten the sailor's cot—
    His bark is bound for home.

HOMEWARD BOUND.

In vain the fragrant spice-groves fling
    Their perfume o'er the tide;
In vain the sparkling ripples sing
    Of the goodly pearls they hide;
Nor earth nor sea a bribe can bring
    To tempt our bark aside!

'Tis thus the storm-beat Christian sails
    The changeful sea of life,
He drifts at the will of the furious gales
    When tempests dark are rife;
And often his very spirit quails
    At the roar of the angry strife.

But hark! the cry is 'Homeward bound!'
    And, see, his visage now
Grows bright beneath the thrilling sound,
    Joy beams upon his brow:
He scatters the waves of care aside,
    Like the bark, with cleaving prow.

'Homeward bound! Homeward bound!'
    My soul, be this thy cry!
Swerve not one inch for their angry sound
    When the storms of life sweep by;
But steer for the light which beams around
    Thy Father's home on high!

TO-DAY AND TO-MORROW.

"Thou art my hope in the day of evil."—JER. xvii. 17.

To-day is full of care :
To-morrow, when it shines,
Shall smooth those wrinkled lines
　　Each brow doth bear ;
For when on Jesus' breast
The weary head shall rest,
　　Sweet peace is there.

To-day sin weaves its chain :
To-morrow, freed from all
Its misery and thrall,
　　Freedom shall reign.
The soul, wash'd in the flood
Of sinless Jesus' blood,
　　Shall know no stain !

TO-DAY AND TO-MORROW.

To-day we mourners weep:
To-morrow hath no tears! (¹)
No gloomy doubts—no fears
    O'er us can sweep:
Clasp'd in their arms above,
The graves of those we love
    No tear-drops steep.

To-day we sow the soil:
To-morrow we shall reap,
If, fainting not, we keep
    True to our toil: (²)
When o'er the boundless plains
The golden harvest reigns,
    How rich the spoil!

To-day we mortals die:
To-morrow knows no death— (³)
Its foul and deadly breath
    Blights not on high;
Each flow'r transplanted there
Shall bloom for ever fair,
    Nor droop—nor die!

---

(1) *Rev.* vii. 17.
(2) *Gal.* vi. 9.   (3) *Rev.* xxi. 4.

DEPARTING IN PEACE.

"Lord now lettest thou thy servant depart in peace."—Luke ii. 29.

The dawn of my life broke in brightness and beauty,
    'Twas beaming with sunshine and fragrant with flow'rs;
'Twas a scene of enjoyment, for pleasure seem'd duty,
    And light-hearted Mirth sped the lingering hours.

But soon the fair morn was by darkness o'erclouded,
    And sin left its stains 'mid its brightness and bloom;
Its pleasures were gone, and its happiness shrouded,
    Its mirth turn'd to sorrow, its sunshine to gloom.

The toys of my childhood no longer delighted—
    The flow'rs that enraptur'd now charm'd me in vain;
The haunts I once loved were forsaken and slighted—
    The scenes that brought pleasure now fill'd me with pain:

For the friends of my youth who once sported beside me,
    Had left me alone in my wilderness-way;
Some lived to neglect me, some learned to deride me,
    And others were torn, like heart-tendrils, away.

DEPARTING IN PEACE.

Thus my spirit grew hard as I sadly detected
   So little on earth of affection and truth;
'Till my conscience within show'd how *I* had neglected,
   And wander'd away from the Guide of my youth.

Then I sorrow'd no more o'er the ties He had broken,
   O'er the twilight around me, so silent and dim;
But I turn'd to that God who in mercy had spoken,
   And shatter'd the fetters which kept me from Him.

Oh, what are earth's friendships, and sunbeams, and flow'rs,
   To the smile of that Saviour my spirit hath found?
How sad and how dark are her sunniest hours
   To the gladness and glory which Jesus surround!

Praise God for the brightness of life's early dawning;
   Praise Him who that brightness thought fit to decrease;
'Twas good I should pass thro' the valley of mourning,
   That my soul might depart to my Saviour in peace.

LOOKING FOR THE EVENING.

"Is there not an appointed time to man upon earth ? are not his days also like the days of an hireling ? As a servant earnestly desireth the shadow, and as an hireling looketh for the reward of his work: So am I made to possess months of vanity, and wearisome nights are appointed to me.—*Job* vii. 1, 2, 3.

Hireling ! why that constant gazing
   Upward to the radiant sky ?
See, the mid-day sun is blazing
   Fiercely from its throne on high:
Toil and heat must yet befall thee—
   Much thy soul must be opprest,
Ere the length'ning shadows call thee
   To thy recompense and rest.

Earnestly and uncomplaining,
   Labor thine appointed hour;
Ev'ry idle wish restraining,
   Putting forth thy utmost pow'r:
Labor on a little longer—
   Toil as in thy Master's sight;
Faith shall make thy spirit stronger—
   Prayer shall make thy burden light.

LOOKING FOR THE EVENING.

Think of Him who watches o'er thee
    With a Father's yearning love;
Ponder on the rest before thee
    In that Father's home above:
Think how Christ himself will meet thee,
    Tenderness in look and voice,—
How those long-lost friends will greet thee,
    Who around his throne rejoice.

Soon shall sunbeams, ling'ring brightly,
    Crimson yonder distant hill;
Ev'ning zephyrs, breathing lightly,
    Thro' the whisp'ring groves shall thrill:
Soon shall twilight mists be blended
    O'er the meadows smiling now;
Soon shalt thou, thy labour ended,
    Wring the moisture from thy brow.

Hireling, see! the shadows lengthen!
    Darkness o'er the landscape low'rs!
May the Holy Spirit strengthen
    For life's solemn closing hours!—
Hireling! happy 'bove all measure,
    Now thy recompense receive;
For tears and toil, delight and pleasure
    Shall thy heav'nly Master give.

NIGHT AND MORNING.

" Weeping may endure for a night, but joy cometh in the morning."—
Psalm. xxx. 5.

Deep was the night of ignorance,
  My spirit which confined;
Wisdom divine no kindling glance
    Shed o'er this darken'd mind:
But, lo! the morning beameth now,
With light and truth around her brow
    In living chaplets twined.

Dreary the painful night of sin,
  Which made my bosom sigh;
No holiness could bloom within—
    The fount of joy was dry:
But, with the morning's crimson flame,
God's holy, blessed Spirit came
    To cleanse and sanctify.

NIGHT AND MORNING.

Dreadful the gloomy night of death,
    When soul and body part;
When fails the feeble, flutt'ring breath,
    And stops the throbbing heart:
But soon the morning light shall break
On Earth's green graves, the dead to wake—
    To heal the mourner's smart.

The night of ignorance is past—
    The night of sin is done!
The night of death—deepest and last—
    Is hast'ning swiftly on;—
'Tis past! O, bliss! beyond the skies,
I see the endless morning rise—
    Rejoice, all night is gone!

PISGAH.

"Get thee up into the top of Pisgah, and lift up thine eyes westward, and northward, and southward, and eastward, and behold it with thine eyes: for thou shalt not go over this Jordan."—*Deut.* iii. 27.

A lone and hoary pilgrim looks
    Forth from a mountain's brow;
He marks the silver-shining brooks
    Which thread the plains below:
He sees the golden sunshine gleam
Upon the fleet and ample stream (¹)
    Where Jordan's waters flow.

Beyond, the purple-cluster'd vine,
    Rich-laden, prostrate lies;
There fertile valleys laugh and shine,
    And feath'ry palm-trees rise;
There, fringing Lebanon's far height,
Tall cedars stand, a goodly sight,
    And tow'r to yonder skies.

---

(1) *Josh.* iii. 15.

PISGAH.

He looks—but sorrow bows his head—
    Sad, yet resign'd his air;
He may but *view*, he may not *tread*
    That promised region fair:
Others shall see those waters part—
Others shall cross with swelling heart (2)
    But *he* will not be there!

An *unknown sepulchre* must hide
    His mouldering remains; (3)
There dews shall fall at eventide—
    Early and latter rains;
But Friendship's tears shall glitter not
Above that lone, mysterious spot,
    Where solemn silence reigns.

O agèd pilgrim, that fair strand
    Which glads thy failing sight,
But typifies the Heav'nly land
    Which sin can never blight;
There, in a better, purer clime,
Freed from the guilt and care of Time,
    Thy day shall know no night. (4)

---

(2) *Josh.* iii. 16.   (3) *Deut.* xxxiv. 6.
(4) *Rev.* xxi. 25, and xxii. 5.

PISGAH.

Thus, often, at the eve of life,
   Before the yawning tomb
Closes the Christian's weary strife,
   And wraps the world in gloom;
God plants the soul on some bold height,
And gives it glorious visions bright
   Of its celestial home:

And, child of God! if He deny
   A goodly portion *here*,
Climb Pisgah's summit, steep and high,
   And look to yonder sphere;
Behold that everlasting plain,
Where bliss, and peace, and glory reign,
   And blush for ev'ry tear.

THE PROMISED LAND.

"When thou hast eaten and art full, then thou shalt bless the Lord thy God for the good land which he hath given thee."—Deuter. viii. 10.

We've trod this earthly wilderness
    For many weary years,
We've tasted Marah's bitterness, (1)
    And wept unnumber'd tears;
But now we're crossing Jordan's stream,
    A glad, triumphant band,
And soon shall share the joys that beam
    In Canaan's promised land.

We fainted for the water-spring,
    A parch'd and thirsty flock,
But God refreshing streams did bring
    From out the cloven rock; (2)
And when our hungry souls did crave
    The true and living bread,
His mercy heav'nly manna gave—
    His famish'd people fed. (3)

---

(1) *Exod.* xv. 23.
(2) *Exod.* xvii. 6. and *Num.* xx. 11.
(3) *Exod.* xvi. 14, 15.

THE PROMISED LAND.

Our shoes and garments failed us not,
    Through all the toilsome way; (⁴)
His loving-kindness ne'er forgot
    Our need from day to day;
And often, when the flame of faith
    Would flicker, pale, and wane,
His Spirit, with reviving breath,
    Would fan that flame again.

As doth a father, full of love,
    Watch o'er a wayward child,
So watch'd He o'er us from above,
    Though weak and sin-defil'd;
Forgiving all our murmurings—
    Our selfishness, and sin,
His saints to Canaan's shore he brings,
    And bids them enter in.

Adieu, thou weary wilderness!
    Our home for many years;
Adieu, to Marah's bitterness!
    Adieu to doubts and tears!
Soon—soon, across death's chilly stream,
    Our ransom'd souls shall stand,
And share the joy and peace that beam
    In Canaan's promised land.

---

(4) *Deut.* xxix. 5.

"IS IT WELL?"

'Is it well with the child? And she answered,'It is well."—2 Kings iv. 26.

O pilgrim! I have heard thy tuneful lyre
    Oft pour upon the night a thrilling strain,
Which seemed thy fainting spirit to inspire
    Throughout its conflict with this world of pain:
Once more, before thy nerveless fingers fail,
Oh, let it breathe upon the passing gale!
                    Is it well?

Thy home and scenes long cherish'd pass away;
    The forms of weeping friends fade from thy view;
Where yonder crimson sunbeams lightly play,
    There is an open grave,—'tis dug for you!
Tears will bedew it oft, and flow'rets fair
Will bloom in fragrant beauty—but declare—
                    Is it well?

"IS IT WELL?"

Pilgrim! thy heavy head sinks wearily—
    Thy closing eyes look filmy, dull, and dim;
Thy parting breath comes short and painfully—
    Above thy pillow bends a phantom grim:
Thy long and toilsome pilgrimage is past—
Oh! say, lest that deep breath should be thy last,—
                      Is it well?

See, thou art sinking 'neath the rising surge
    Of death's untried, unfathomable sea;
Her dark and restless waves a mournful dirge,
    With melancholy cadence, sing for thee:
Oh, ere those rising billows 'bove thee roll,
Say, I beseech thee, say, departing soul!
                      Is it well?

" At peace through Christ, no earthly lyre can tell
    The ecstacy of bliss which thrills me now;
Heav'n's highest joys my heaving bosom swell—
    Its wreaths of glory press upon my brow:
Though home and weeping friends no more I see,
A home no grief can cloud is waiting me:—
                      It is well!

"IS IT WELL?"

"Yes, I am weary; but on Jesus' breast
   I can this aching head lay gently down:
Toilsome the path, but oh, how sweet the rest!
   How passing beautiful the fadeless crown!
My grave is meet for me, I for my grave;
He bids me come who died to bless and save:
Death's dark'ning waves may round me surge and sing
Fast to the Living Rock my soul doth cling:—
                      It is well!"

DETACHED POEMS.

DETACHED POEMS.

THE WIDOW OF NAIN.

"Now when He came nigh to the gate of the city, behold, there was a dead man carried out, the only son of his mother, and she was a widow; and much people of the city was with her."—Luke vii. 12.

The scene was fair, as when o'er Eden's bowers
The sun first shone upon the new-born flowers,
And youthful Nature glow'd beneath his eye
In all the charms of pristine purity.
The earth, array'd in Summer's gorgeous dress,
Blush'd, like a bride, with conscious loveliness,
Whom twining flowers with varied bloom enwreathe,
And balmy odours round her person breathe.
The azure sky shone tranquilly and pure,
Nor did the gloom of passing cloud obscure
The radiant lustre of the orb of day,
Which lit the landscape with its glorious ray;

THE WIDOW OF NAIN.

Kiss'd the fair streamlet as it stole along,
Breathing in accents soft its murm'ring song,
Till each bright ripple, as it onward roll'd,
Bore on its crest a sparkling fringe of gold;
Whilst feather'd choristers, from vocal throats,
Pour'd forth on air their sweet, melodious notes,
Which perfum'd zephyrs wafted high above,
A grateful anthem to the God of love.

But Nain was sad, though all was peace on high,
And pity dimm'd each sympathizing eye;
A form belov'd from earth had passed away,
A widow'd parent's only hope and stay.
From out the city pour'd the sombre train,
And wound its way across the smiling plain;
With solemn movement, and with muffled tread,
They slowly bare him to his earthy bed.
There were sad looks around that lowly bier,—
To many hearts that silent form was dear;
Full many a sob burst from each kindred breast,
Full many a cheek in sorrow's garb was drest.
Yet was there one, bound by a closer tie,
Whose very soul seem'd wrung with agony;
Whose pallid brow and heav'n-directed glance
Pourtray'd a grief too deep for utterance:
Of all earth's loves her's was the purest flame,—
To mourn a son that widow'd mother came.

THE WIDOW OF NAIN.

Declin'd he with a lengthen'd life's decay,
His features wither'd, and his thin locks grey,—
His tott'ring frame by age and weakness bent,
His senses numb'd, his failing vigour spent?
Fell he, as Nature's fading leaves do fall,
When milder climes the swallows southward call;
When chilly winds and weather damp and drear,
Proclaim, with voice distinct, the winter near?
Ah, no! that form was yet unmarr'd by Time,
Yet unexpanded into manhood's prime.
He scarce had spent a third of that brief span
Which wisely bounds the pilgrimage of man;
Before him still, veil'd in the future, lay
An unknown space, which Hope's inviting ray
Fill'd up with pictures, welcome to the eyes,
Of earthly bliss and converse with the skies;
Pictures and promises too bright for Time,
And only realized in purer clime.
Thus in the very vigour of his life,
When, full of hope, he armed him for the strife,
Upon the goodly prospect fell a cloud,
And Death and darkness wrapt him in their shroud.

With what deep joy that mother hail'd his birth!
To her there was not such a babe on earth;
So soft, so pure, so innocent and fair,—
Yes, ev'ry beauty seemed concentred there.

THE WIDOW OF NAIN.

Fondly she gazed with love-illumin'd eyes,
And view'd each morn fresh dawning charms arise;
Bedew'd him oft with sweetest tears of joy,
As tender vigils midnight hours employ;
And fervent pray'rs, faith-winged, ascend above,
Invoking thence a watchful Father's love;—
That as the child advanced into the youth,
He still might seek, and serve, and love the truth.

And when God summon'd from her side to part,
The dear companion of her home and heart,
And left her weak, unaided womanhood
Alone to battle with the world's dark flood;
E'en then, within the cup her lips must press,
A branch of love allay'd its bitterness: [1]
The dead yet lived in his surviving son,
Husband and child she now embraced in one;
And in her offspring, suffered to remain,
She found a balm to soothe her spirit's pain.
For as the soul, of one lov'd thing bereft,
Clings closer still round those which yet are left,
So these two treasures all her woes beguil'd,—
Her hopes of Heav'n, her dear and winning child.
Like some sweet flow'ret on a barren isle,
He cheer'd her lonely bosom with his smile,

---

[1] Exod. xv. 25.

THE WIDOW OF NAIN.

Which beam'd upon her with enliv'ning ray,
And chased the gloom of darkling care away;
Inspired her bosom with a holy peace,
And bade Affliction's flowing rills to cease.

Perchance her deep, her fond maternal love,
Trespass'd too much on that of Him above,—
To whom the soul's devotion first is due,
The ' God of love,' the ever just and true,—
And He, her wand'ring, earthly love to chide,
Bore him away who turn'd her heart aside;
For Death's stern hand, ere it commenced to bloom,
Pluck'd the fair flow'r to wither in the tomb:
Eclipsed the sunshine in her widow'd breast,
Now pierced with anguish and with gloom opprest.
Still clave that heart, sore stricken, to its God,
And kiss'd the hand which grasp'd the chast'ning rod,
Beseeching grace, whate'er might be His will,
To bow her soul in meek submission still.
The tear-worn cheek, the deep and choking sob,
The anguish'd bosom's agonizing throb,—
Who would reprove emotions Nature gave?
When e'en the Saviour wept above the grave;
Let fall those precious crystals from His eye,
In silent grief, o'er cold mortality.
Slowly she moved amid the funeral train,
To soothe her pangs no earthly hopes remain;

THE WIDOW OF NAIN.

She look'd on him she loved,—lo! lifeless clay,—
The soul had burst its bonds and flown away:
She turn'd her gaze to Heaven's extended plain,
Her only solace,—'There we meet again!'

But there was One amid that silent throng
To whom all pow'rs did bow, all might belong :
Whose heart was tender to the tears of woe,
And ever yearned sweet comfort to bestow.
One who could bid dark ocean's waves 'Be still!'
Or rouse their billows at His sovereign will;
Could bid the sick forsake their weary bed,
To heap thanksgivings on His gracious head :
Could bid the lame amid the dance proclaim
The might and glory of Messiah's name;
Could bid the dumb their new-found voices raise
In loud hosannas, and in songs of praise :
Could, with a word, chill life's warm-flowing tide,
Or bid the tomb unfold its caverns wide,
Yield back its occupant, to light restored,
And own the sway of an Almighty Lord.
That loving Being could not pass her by,
But, with compassion beaming in His eye,
"*Weep not*," He says, as softly drawing near,
He lays his hand upon the dead man's bier.
His visage shines, illum'd by Pity's ray,
Like fair Gennesareth at close of day,

THE WIDOW OF NAIN.

When o'er its bosom sunbeams smile adieu,
And not a ripple waves its surface blue.
Awed by His aspect of celestial grace,
The bearers cease their slow and mournful pace;
To Him at once their wond'ring eyes they raise,
And e'en the chief of mourners turns to gaze.
"*Weep not!*" those accents thrill her wounded heart,
And to her soul tumultuous hopes impart,—
Hopes she can scarce define, much less express,
Yet still they seem to whisper happiness.
But, hark! that voice again breaks on the ear,
And e'en the dead the loud appeal must hear,—
"*Young man, I say to thee, Arise!*"—the strife
Is ended now, and re-awaken'd life
Hath burst the frozen bonds of icy death,
And summon'd back the once departed breath.
The soul, recall'd, returns with quick'ning flame,
To warm and animate that earthy frame;
Along his veins careers the crimson tide,
And once again those bright eyes open wide;
Whilst o'er that pale, emaciated cheek,
Beams forth once more health's rosy-tinted streak.
'The dead rose up, and sat, and spake!'
The stoutest hearts with awe and terror quake,
As He, who broke Death's adamantine chain,
Back to the parent gives the child again.

THE WIDOW OF NAIN.

Now from her soul rolls sorrow's gloom away,
As morning mists before the dawn of day;
Whilst sweet emotions in her bosom swell,
Of bliss too deep-felt for her lips to tell;
But silv'ry tear-drops stealing down her cheek,
With silent eloquence her gladness speak.
Fast to her breast she clasps her risen child,
And worships Him who on her rapture smil'd.

Now thronging multitudes, with loud acclaim,
Pour forth the praises of Messiah's name;
" A prophet! lo, a prophet!" is the cry,
" God hath come down from majesty on high!
Hath visited His own, His chosen race,
And ope'd the fountains of His heav'nly grace!"
Men, women, children, lisping infants, raise
The mingled shout, and swell the note of praise,
Till, rising high, it rends the concave sky,
And rolls before the star-thron'd Deity!

THE WORK AND THE WORKERS.

" Why stand ye here all the day idle?"—Matt. xx. 6.

A glorious privilege 'tis to live
In an age like this! when God doth give
The right to labor to one and all,
To rich and to poor,—to great and small;
When all may find something to do or dare,
In freeing this world from sin and care.

Shame on the lazy, loitering loon,
Who can twiddle his thumbs from morn till noon,
Whilst every one with the soul of a man
Is pushing along to the battle's van;
And striving to leave his mark on an age,
That shall proudly gleam upon History's page!
Shame on the languid miss, who can loll
Half her days, like a delicate doll,
In an easy chair, with a novel or play,
Whilst the rest of her sex are working away;
When God has bestowed on her youth and health,
And time, and talents, and, may be, wealth,—

THE WORK AND THE WORKERS.

The name of a *woman* who would fling
Away on that trifling, trick'd out thing?

Surely if we have a single spark
Of the goodness of God in our nature dark,
We cannot be destin'd to travel through
This work-day world with nothing to do,—
With nought but the things of sense or sin
To draw out the pow'rs our breast within:
There must be something to do or plan,
For each feeling woman and true-hearted man!
Are all the noble and loving schemes
For the welfare of men, but glowing themes
On which we may talk with tripping tongue,
Whilst not a nerve is for effort strung?
Are they not rare opportunities given
To discipline souls for the courts of Heaven?
Noble engines to work God's will,
To forward good, and to vanquish ill?

Wherever we turn, wherever we stand,
There is plenty of work all ready to hand:
We may aid the wants of our fellow-man,
And mend his lot as best we can;
We may save from the tavern, the treadmill, or worse,
The souls that still linger beneath the curse;

THE WORK AND THE WORKERS.

We may seek them out in the haunts of sin,
Where squalor and misery lurk within;
We may lead them forth to the light of day,
And give their slumb'ring powers full play;
We may build them Churches, and found them Schools,
Check evil habits by loving rules;
We may cleanse from weeds the mental soil,
Procure them books and honest toil;
We may give them a place in the social scale,
And send them forth, with a cheering gale,
To plough the stormy sea of life,
And fight, like men, the Christian's strife.

But if there is nought at *hand* to strain
Your nerves, look forth on Earth's wide plain!
The harvest of God is tall and white,
It waits but the sickle, keen and bright,
And its goodly sheaves will soon be seen
Where the reaper's busy feet have been.
" Where are the Reapers?" Hark, the cry!
Shall that thrilling call meet no reply?
Oh! pray that the Lord may quickly send
Faithful reapers, ready to bend
Their willing backs the fields to sweep,—
A noble harvest of souls to reap.
And, idle friend, with nothing to do,
May be *the Lord hath a sickle for you!*

THE WORK AND THE WORKERS.

If you are a woman, you've fingers ten,
More taper, 'tis true, than those of men,
But able to furnish a mountain of '*work*,'
When the spirit is ready,—unwilling to shirk.
If you are a man, you have money to spare,
It may be perchance a goodly share ;
At least you've the strength to carry through
Whatever your hand may find to do.
Stand not in the market, then, day by day,
Idly droning your life away,
But look around, the world is wide,
And the good and the great work side by side :
Yet is there room, enough and to spare,
For all who are willing to labor there.
From every grade and stage of life,
Christ's people flock to the noble strife ;
Both heaven and earth re-echo and ring,
With the deeds they do, and the strains they sing ;
Soon, soon, shall the powers of darkness yield,
And the banner of victory float o'er the field !

Oh ! take your place 'mid the sons of toil,
Be yours the conflict,—yours the spoil !
Labor may weary and moisten now,
But soon shall the palm-wreath bind your brow.
Man may scorn, oppose, and frown,
Mock at your efforts, and cry them down,

THE WORK AND THE WORKERS.

But let them bark and bray,—what then?
God is your judge, not selfish men!
The work is His, and none shall stay,
Work on in faith, and wait, and pray.
And, oh, when your earthly course is run,
How welcome your Master's words ;—" Well done!
Well done, laborer, true to me!
Long have I watched and followed thee :
I know thy labor, thy works, thy love,
I have treasured them up in my book above ;
And none shall perish, no, not one,
Of the noble deeds thy hand hath done!
They shall bloom on, as the fruits of faith,
When thy perishing body lies cold in death ;
And thou shalt be mine, for ever and aye,
In the shining realms of eternal day!"

Oh! who would perish and pass away
From earth, like a clod of kindred clay?
With not one streak of light to mark
His selfish path through this world so dark.
Oh! who would sink, unmiss'd, unknown,
To a grave unmark'd by flower or stone?
With none to love him, and none to shed
A tear o'er the turf above him spread ;
With none to breathe or bless his name,
When the worms have fed on his fleshly frame.

THE WORK AND THE WORKERS.

Oh! who would stand at the throne on high,
Where the Lord of glory the world shall try,—
Where the angel-throng sweet strains shall sing,
As the faithful servants their witness bring,—
And there, 'mid the slothful and lost, be found
With his God-given talents still ' napkin bound?'

Up, up, then, brother! and take thy stand
'Mid the workmen of Christ, with head or hand;
Blush not to be seen 'mid His laborers true,
But blush, if you will, that you've nothing to do!
Blush that you care for nought but self,
For this world's pleasure, or pomp, or pelf,—
That, out of the thousands thine eyes can see,
Man, woman, nor child owes aught to thee!

THE DEATH-SIGNAL.

On the broad, deep blue of Ocean's breast,
    May a gallant bark be seen;
With the sinking sun, she steers due west,
    With a trail of foaming sheen:
Her snow-white sails abroad are spread
    To the breeze that whispers by;
The bunting flutters overhead,
    But that flag is half-mast high.

The captain had one blooming child,
    A motherless, fair-haired boy;
Like the breeze of ocean, free and wild,
    His sailor father's joy:
Of the whole ship's crew the blithest he,—
    The lov'd of every eye;
But now he lies all silently,
    And the flag is half-mast high.

THE DEATH-SIGNAL.

That ransom'd soul is fled and gone,
    With a low and parting wail,
But still the bounding bark bears on
    Before the fresh'ning gale;
Still, still the curling billows foam,
    And the sea-bird glances by,
Though dark is the captain's cabin-home,
    And his flag is half-mast high.

A shrouded form lies on the deck,
    And the silent crew stand round;
The ship might be a forsaken wreck,
    So hush'd is every sound:
But the voice of pray'r is on the wind,
    And a low, half-utter'd cry,—
One passenger is left behind,
    And the flag is half-mast high.

That bark on many a sea shall sail,
    And brave out many a storm;
But ne'er will her captain's cheek be pale
    As it was o'er that dying form:
Whilst oft he will think of the far-off shore,
    With a yearning and a sigh,
Where he'll meet his child, when the flag once more
    Of his bark waves half-mast high.

THE EMIGRANT'S DEPARTURE.

A Scene in Ulster. A.D. 1853.

Wailing aloud, a weeping band
    Stood by a lonely road;
In sorrow was clasp'd each trembling hand,
    And glittering tear-drops flow'd:
Women were there, and their piercing cry
    Came sad on the balmy air,
Though the birds sang sweet, and the noontide sky
    Smiled soft on the landscape fair.

Thus far they'd trudg'd from their native place,
    Till their weary feet were sore,
A kiss,—a sob,—one last embrace,—
    And the parting scene was o'er:
The parents' grief was shed o'er a son,
    O'er a brother the sister's tear,
And perchance in the group there yet was one
    To whom he was still more dear.

THE EMIGRANT'S DEPARTURE.

Onward he goes, but the mournful swell
    Of that cry still greets his ear,—
Soundeth it not like a heart-rung knell
    For a lost one, lov'd and dear?
And perchance it is, for an only child
    Is leaving his early home,—
His grave may be the ocean wild,
    And his shroud the curling foam.

He pauses again for a farewell sight
    Of that sad but faithful band;
The road forsaken, they've climb'd the height,
    In a clustering group they stand:
They wave the hand as a last adieu,
    They strain the aching eye,—
May the pray'r they breathe, as he fades from view,
    Find grace with One on high!

A blessing on thee, exiled lad,—
    A blessing night and day!
Well may thy home-sick heart be sad,
    As thou tread'st thy lonely way:
Though slow thy step, and dim thine eye,—
    Though tears bedew thy cheek,
Blush not at the glance of the passer-by,
    Nor fear he will deem thee weak.

THE EMIGRANT'S DEPARTURE.

Oh no, not so! he will honor thee more
    For that pure and simple sign
Of love, than if thou the proudest wore
    In the gem resplendent mine:
Then brush not away that tear, fond boy!
    In truth it becomes thee well;
And oh! in thy after hours of joy,
    Remember for whom it fell.

Veil, veil, sweet Erin, thy tearful face,
    And thy tuneful harp unstring!
Whilst sad are the homes of thy chosen race,
    Can its joyous changes ring?
Still, feel in thy bosom a glow of pride,—
    Though the rich and great may scorn,
The fervent love of thy children tried
    Would honor the noblest born!

CHIMES OF THE SEA.

Born in the earliest dawn of Time,
    I shall be till Time is o'er;
I sing my songs in every clime,
    And compass every shore:
From North to South, from East to West,
    My giant waves are hurl'd;
Was there ever a monarch like me, possess'd
    Of more than half a world?

I'm grave, I'm gay, I shout or sing,
    As it suits my varying mind,
But, whatever my state, I wonder bring
    To the hearts of human kind:
And when first I show to stranger eyes,
    The majesty girding me,
How thrills his heart as he wildly cries
    "The sea! The sea! The sea!"

CHIMES OF THE SEA.

The broad Atlantic's my hall of pride,
    A myriad serfs I own,
And at every ebb of my mighty tide,
    They gather about my throne;
They come, the near and the far away,
    From cave, and cliff, and tower,
From golden fields and gardens gay,
    And many a lady's bower.

In the fair Pacific I love to smile,
    And lull my waves to rest,
While many a glittering coral isle
    Gleams bright on my heaving breast:
But far away in the Northern seas,
    I am chill'd to the very soul,
For the icy winds my heart's blood freeze
    As I circle the silent Pole.

I bask beneath Italian skies,—
    I muse by classic Greece,
And scarce can an angry feeling rise
    'Mid scenes so full of peace;
And even I, over Glory's grave,
    A tear can almost shed,
As I flow with bright and placid wave
    By the 'city of the dead.'

CHIMES OF THE SEA.

I wander among the Hebrides,
    Down Staffa's solemn aisles,
And dear to my soul is the passing breeze
    From Iona's sacred piles;
For it whispers of ages dark and drear,
    Of a well nigh pagan night,
When outcast Truth found a refuge here,
    And shone as a beacon bright.

Around Columbia's rocks I roar,
    And wealthy Hindostan;
And many a bleak and barren shore,
    Untrod by the foot of man:
But Albion's isle I guard with awe,
    For I honor her bulwarks white,
And woe to the foe who defies her law,
    When she rules for truth and right!

Wherever my endless waters foam,
    Her red cross flag's unfurl'd,
As proudly she bears to her island home
    The wealth of a teeming world:
And scatters abroad, with bounteous hand,
    The blessings her God hath given,—
'The freedom of thought of her own free land,
    And the faith which lights to Heaven.'

Spain, Venice, and Carthage, where are they?
    And where are the wreaths they won?
They are silent all, in Fame's decay,—
    Their course of glory's run;
But a mightier monarch now wears my crown,
    For it graces Britannia's head,—
May her garments of state be Truth and Renown,
    Till her mission be nobly sped!

HAVELOCK'S GRAVE.*

Where does the mighty Havelock sleep?
  Who, with avenging sword,
Like some fierce whirlwind o'er the deep,
  Burst through the heathen horde;
Who bore, amid dark Battle's frown,
Relief to Lucknow's leaguer'd town,
  And vanish'd hope restor'd.

---

* This poem was written on the perusal of the following extract from the Indian Correspondence of the "London Times," communicated by Dr. Russell. It subsequently appeared that the disturbed state of the country, and the desire of the present Sir H. Havelock to erect a monument to his father's memory, deterred the public from paying that due attention to the hero's grave which they would otherwise gratefully have done. A suitable testimonial has since been raised above his remains; but his earnest piety and military fame are his most lasting memorials. None could more truly have said
"Exegi monumentum ære perennius!"
Hor. Car. III. 30.

" I wish I could say to the people of England, who lamented Havelock so deeply, that the grave of their chosen one is worthily marked, or that its present condition is worthy of the remains which lie there, or of the country. When I visited the Alumbagh, where Sir Henry Havelock was hurriedly interred in the march of the relieved garrison out of Lucknow, I saw, in the unclean garden ground of the place, open to natives, cattle, and dogs, a shallow sinking in the ground the size of a grave—and it was a grave—and just over it, rudely carved by a soldier's hand on the trunk of a tree, could be traced the letter " H." And this is the grave and the inscription of Sir Henry Havelock!"—*Times, March* 1859.

HAVELOCK'S GRAVE.

Where sleeps the Christian soldier now—
    Now that his course is sped,
And Fame has wreath'd her fav'rite's brow ?
    Where rests his weary head
Who sought not only man's applause,
But in Humanity's high cause
    His life blood freely shed ?

Lies he beneath some sacred pile,
    Amid the good and great,
In solemn, still cathedral aisle,
    In military state ;
Where England's sons and daughters fair
Oft love to linger, tearful, there,
    To muse upon his fate ?

Lies he, as heroes lay of old,
    'Neath some majestic mound,
Rear'd by the noble and the bold
    Where silence reigns around ;
Where friend and foe with rev'rence meet,
And feel the spot beneath their feet
    Is consécrated ground ?

HAVELOCK'S GRAVE.

No, pilgrim! seek no solemn pile,
    No mound on battle plain,
No dim and still cathedral aisle,—
    Thy search would be but vain:
But hither turn thy longing eyes,
Draw near in mute and sad surprise,
    With mingled grief and pain.

Behold this rude, unhallow'd spot,
    This unclean, open space,—
Nay, pilgrim, pause—despise it not—
    Turn not aside thy face;
Though dogs and cattle prowl around,
That 'shallow sinking in the ground'
    Is Havelock's resting place!

This tree that lifts its friendly head
    To shelter and to save,
Serves both as tombstone for the dead
    And tablet for the brave;
Upon its bark one letter stands,
Inscribed by fond and faithful hands,
    To mark the hero's grave.

HAVELOCK'S GRAVE.

What though his bones neglected lie,
    Unguarded and alone ;
What though no rival artists vie
    To rear the sculptur'd stone:
He needs no monumental state,
Which makes man neither good nor great
    Before th' Almighty's throne.

His name's a cherish'd 'household word,'
    Enshrin'd in English hearts ;
Where'er its honor'd sound is heard,
    Full many a tear-drop starts :
His fame—his pure, unsullied fame,
Shall burn with never-dying flame
    Till England's glory parts !

But, oh ! more blest, more happy still,—
    Long ere his strifes were o'er,
He look'd to Zion's holy hill
    From Earth's attractive shore ;
Now, risen on the wings of Faith,
His soul has cross'd the stream of Death,
    And lives for evermore !

MEMORIAL OF MACAULAY.

"Vel pace vel bello clarum fieri licet: et qui fecere, et qui facta aliorum scripsere, multi laudantur."—Sall. Cat. cap. 3.

Bereavèd Britain, weep! for thou
    Hast lost a noble son,
With wreaths all fresh upon his brow,
    The wreaths by genius won;
His glory, by no cloud o'ercast,
Resplendent to the very last,
    Has set like mid-day sun!

He lies amid the noble dead,
    Whose names can never die
Till Time his weary course has sped,
    And shines Eternity:
The same high honors round him close,
His cherish'd bones with theirs repose,—
    Methinks I see him lie!

MEMORIAL OF MACAULAY.

Above Macaulay's honor'd tomb,
    Three figures seem to stand:
Sweet flowers, with never-dying bloom,
    Fall from each quiv'ring hand:
On him are bent their earnest eyes,
For him their bosoms heave with sighs,—
    Who form this mournful band?

There History with her scroll is seen,
    With pensive look and sage,
Whilst many a tear-drop with its sheen
    Spangles the glorious page;
That page o'er which her child has thrown
A light, a halo all his own,
    To shine through many an age.

There Poesy's graceful figure droops,
    Her sweet-ton'd lyre unstrung;
There Eloquence in silence stoops,
    For sorrow chains his tongue:
Long shall they deeply grieve for him,
Long shall their tearful eyes be dim,
    And mournful notes be sung!

MEMORIAL OF MACAULAY.

Bard and *Historian*, who hast spread
    Before a nation's gaze
Bright pages, which have o'er thee shed
    Such beams of *human* praise:
May thine own history, writ above,
Beam bright with Christian faith and love,
    And angel anthems raise!

ON THE DECEASE OF THE PRINCE CONSORT.

A.D. 1861. ÆT. 41.

"Quis desiderio sit pudor aut modus
Tam cari capitis?"
Hor. Car. Lib. I. 24.

A nation weeps—and why?
A brother hath departed,
Noble, and Christian-hearted,
   To bliss on high:
A prince hath past from earth,
Whose deeds of love and worth
   Shall never die.

A nation weeps—and why?
A bright and precious gem,
From England's diadem,
   Is now laid by:
A pure and gifted mind
No more shall lead mankind
   To triumphs high.

ON THE DECEASE OF THE PRINCE CONSORT.

    A nation weeps—and why?
Each man hath lost a friend;
The poor, one who could bend
    With pitying eye,
To learn and meet their need
With kindly word and deed,
    And sympathy.

    A nation weeps—and why?
In its lov'd Queen's distress,
A *husband's* tenderness
    It would supply;
As grief her spirit stirs,
Mingling its tears with hers,
    No eye is dry.

    Thus England's grief flows on,
Above that silent tomb
Where fondest mem'ries bloom:
    She weeps with one
Whose *deeper* grief she shares,
Yet speak their mingled pray'rs—
    "*God's will be done!*"

THE FAITHFUL STEWARD.*

"Inasmuch as ye have done it unto one of the least of these my brethren, ye have done it unto me."—*Matt.* xxv. 40.

Steward of Christ! when cank'ring rust
Hath dimm'd Earth's glory and her gold;
When, sleeping 'neath the gath'ring dust,
Thy frame lies tenantless and cold;
When thou art summon'd to resign
That mighty stewardship of thine,
Then shall thy faithfulness be told.

---

* Written in commemoration of Mr. George Peabody's parting donation of £150,000 to the poor of London, in which city this Christian-minded merchant amassed his vast fortune. The donor was born in Danvers, Massachusetts, U. S., and in humble circumstances.

THE FAITHFUL STEWARD.

Unnumber'd sons of wretchedness
    Shall breathe in pray'r thy cherish'd name,—
Shall tell how, in their deep distress,
    Thy bounty quicken'd Hope's dull flame ;
When o'er life's dark and troubled stream
A comforting and cheering beam,
    Like smile from heaven, sweetly came.

" I was an hungred,—thou didst fill
    This wasted frame with strength'ning meat ! "
" Parch'd were these fev'rish lips until
    Thy love provided cordial sweet ! "
" I was a homeless child, and bare,
Till, warmly clothed and housed with care,
    Thy mercy took me from the street ! "

Oh ! when before the judgment throne,
    How dear to Christ—how dear to thee,
(Though ne'er for sin it can atone,)
    Shall that unfailing witness be ;
When thousands rise to call thee blest,
And thus, with mingled voice, attest
    Thy love and thy fidelity !

THE FAITHFUL STEWARD.

Ye men of rank, or monied worth!
    Whose bursting granaries enfold
The riches of the teeming earth,—
    Whose iron coffers hoard her gold:
Circled by all wealth can command,
Soon will your Lord account demand
    Of ev'ry talent you may hold.

Remember, then, whose love did bless
    Your patient labour, year by year,—
Who crown'd each effort with success,
    Outstripp'd each hope, allay'd each fear:
Freely for Christ let that be spent
Which He for Time has only *lent*,
    And lay not up your treasure here!

Should future bickerings arise,
    Or varying int'rests clash and jar;
Should o'er the calm and radiant skies
    The threat'ning clouds be spread afar,
And Britain and Columbia stand,
Sternly opposed, with sword in hand,
    Intent on fratricidal war:

THE FAITHFUL STEWARD.

Woe be to her whose cursed brand
    Shall first be stained with human gore!
Shall first dissever that blest band
    Which knits together each far shore,
Where, pleading claims of brotherhood,
Are heard on either side the flood
    The prayers of Britain's poor.

ON VISITING THE TOMB OF THE LATE REV. J. B.

OB. A. D. 1855.

Here the Friend—the Husband—the Father sleeps,
   Where the grass is fresh and green,
But the lonely widow sighs and weeps
   Where the billows roll between;

And each orphan bears, in her chasten'd breast,
   A gap she will strive in vain
To fill, till she meets, in eternal rest,
   With that dear-lov'd form again.

Their tears cannot dew the sacred stone—
   Nor their deep sighs murmur there—
Nor can that spot, so far and lone,
   Re-echo their broken pray'r.

ON VISITING THE TOMB OF THE LATE REV. J. B.

The dwellings of strangers are gather'd round—
    Not a kinsman's home is seen—
But, say! will no sorrowing form be found,
    Which oft to that spot hath been?

Will Memory bring no mourner there,
    To pour at that lonely shrine
A tribute tear, or a simple pray'r,
    When the sun's bright beams decline?

Will the snow be spread from day to day
    Round his silent resting place,
And no friendly foot, ere it melts away,
    Leave a single friendly trace?

Ah, yes! though the world hath hard, cold hearts,
    Yet they are not *all* so dead,
But some will grieve when a friend departs,
    And visit his lowly bed:

So, often here will the fond few stray,
    Who knew and could feel his worth
Who now, till the dawn of a brighter day,
    Sleeps on in the womb of Earth!

ON VISITING THE TOMB OF THE LATE REV. J. B.

And some, perchance, in the sacred fane,
    Who have heard his accents flow,
Will fancy they hear him oft again,
    Though his form be cold and low;

And bear abroad in their after life,
    Through his means, the Christian's sign,
' A heart that loves, 'mid a world of strife,
    To muse upon things divine.'

But chiefly the poor, and friendless old,
    Will oft to this spot repair,—
To the tomb of a friend, whose heart and gold
    Could never withstand their pray'r.

Then think not he slumbers *forgotten* here—
    That his name 's like a fallen star,—
There are bosoms that cherish it fondly *near*,
    And many that love it *afar!*

THE PIONEERS.*

Alas! for the daring spirits,
  Now past from earth away,
Whose noble forms are resting
  Beneath their kindred clay;
Who, spent with toil and hunger,
  Lay calmly down to die,
With none but God above them
  To catch their latest sigh.

Forth went those desert wand'rers,
  Steadfast, and true, and bold,
As ever beaded pilgrim
  Set forth in days of old;
Forth went they, in their manhood,
  To dare the trackless wild,
But on their safe returning
  No friends looked forth and smiled.

---

* A tribute to the memory of Burke and Wills, who perished whilst exploring the interior of the continent of Australia, A. D. 1861.

THE PIONEERS.

Their gaze was on the future,
   When, 'neath those glowing skies,
And 'mid those tangled marshes,
   Fair villages shall rise:
When farms and peaceful homesteads
   Shall shine and nestle there,
And lowing herds and reapers
   Make music on the air.

They dreamed not then, those doomed ones,
   That they from earth must pass,
Ere another summer's breezes
   Should wave the blooming grass;
They saw not those wan figures
   Fall, silent, one by one,—
They saw not those stark bodies
   Lie festering in the sun.

Across the fertile regions,
   With ruddy corn now spread,
Some straggling forms first wander'd
   With slow and weary tread;
Athwart the seething ocean,
   Which guards the golden shore,
Some bolder hands first ventured,
   To seek the precious ore.

THE PIONEERS.

Oft, as the hosts of Commerce
    O'er earth go marching on,
Some whitening bones will show us
    Another outpost won;
Yet will each bolder spirit
    Still ever seek the van,
Till desert,—prairie,—forest,
    Confess the sway of man.

So in the path of learning,
    Of Science, Liberty,
Will minds of highest mettle
    The foremost strive to be;
What though they fail of reaching
    Their grand and lofty prize,
At least their prostrate bodies
    Shall help mankind to rise.

Then hail to the noble vanguard—
    The world's brave pioneers!
All honor to their courage,—
    To their memory our tears!
Theirs is the suffering hardship,
    The seed-time and the toil:
For those who may come after
    The harvest and the spoil.

THE PIONEERS.

Shall we, who reap their sowing,
    Think lightly of their dust?
Nay, gather it in silence,
    Deem it a solemn trust:
And let a fitting tribute
    Above their tomb be seen,
Whilst a grateful people's record
    Preserves their memory green.

INSCRIPTION FOR A TIME-PIECE.

As oft you gaze upon my face
And watch each moment's rapid pace,
Let every 'tick' a warning be—
How brief the time allow'd to thee!

And let each fleeting hour be fraught
With holy deed or heavenward thought,
That, when the hands of Time are still,
Eternal joy thy soul may fill!

FINIS.

www.ingramcontent.com/pod-product-compliance
Lightning Source LLC
Chambersburg PA
CBHW031440160426
43195CB00010BB/799